Coming Back to Learning

A handbook for adults

Monica Brand, Eileen De'Ath,
Tessa Doe & Helen Evans

Lifetime Careers

Coming Back to Learning – Reprinted 2002

Published by Lifetime Careers Publishing, 7 Ascot Court,
White Horse Business Park, Trowbridge BA14 0XA

© Lifetime Careers Wiltshire Ltd, 2000

ISBN: 1 902876 07 5

No part of this publication may be copied or reproduced, stored in a retrieval system or transmitted in any form or by any means electronic or mechanical or by photocopying or recording without prior permission of the publishers.

Printed and bound by Cromwell Press, Trowbridge

Cover design by Jane Norman

Text design by Murray Marshall & Jacki Ciereszko

Cartoons by Mark Cripps

Acknowledgements

We would like to thank the following for their assistance in finding people willing to tell their stories for our profiles: Mandy Hamilton of New College Swindon; Samantha Willis of Upham Road Computer Centre, Swindon College; Toni Andrews of Spring Skills and Janet Stanger of the Education Department at HM Prison, Erlestoke. Thanks especially to all those adult learners who were willing to share their experiences with us.

Our acknowledgements also to Paul Stirner, the author of *Coming Back to Education, 1994*, which provided the basis for this book.

Contents

Introduction 7

1 Why learn? 13

2 Sources of advice and guidance 27

3 Ways to learn 41

4 The qualification maze 51

5 Finding the right provider 71

6 Paying your way 103

7 Making your choice 129

8 Taking the plunge 139

9 Building on your learning 155

Publishers' addressess 165

Index 167

Coming Back to Learning

Introduction

Just to inspire you ...

Christina Palmer

'I felt I should write and share my new-found experience as a mature student.

Having raised my children to an age of independence, I found myself looking at my future and not liking what I saw. So I took the plunge and enrolled on an Access course.

First day nerves nearly made me turn and run, but once I met everyone and realised that we were all in the same boat, I did feel more at ease. Well, I did return the next day!

I found that the teachers are, in fact, human, pleasant and very helpful (not what I remembered from school) and with their help, and the support from my new-found friends, I really hope to complete this course.

This Access course offers a varied range of subjects which enable you to go on in your chosen career. It hasn't been easy and, at times, I really have felt like giving up. But an important lesson, which I learned fast, is: when in trouble seek help. They really are there to help us all; they want us to complete this course as much as we do. They give you the confidence to realise that you're not stupid and that you are able to complete this course.

> *I have made many new friends, gained lots of confidence and improved my academic skills beyond belief. I really feel that, having survived this course, my dream will come true of enrolling for a Diploma in nursing.*
>
> *Even if I inspire just one person to go to college and enjoy being there, it will have been worth writing this piece. Go on, give it a go! It's really not as bad as you think. If a woman of thirty with three children can cope, so can you.'*

More and more adults are returning to study or training - some through necessity, as their knowledge and skills become outdated, some through an ambition to improve their prospects, and some for personal challenge and enjoyment. We are in an age of lifelong learning.

Concerns among employers about skills shortages led the Government to set the current targets for learning back in 1995. By 2002 they want 50% of adults (in or seeking employment and aged between 18 and retirement age) to have qualifications at level 3 (that's two A levels or equivalent) and 28% to be qualified to level 4 (HND- or degree-level). There is also a learning participation target for all 16-69 year-olds, which is to reduce by 7% the 26% of adults who have not taken part in any kind of learning in the past three years.

Progress towards meeting these targets is encouraging. In 1999, 45.8% of adults had reached level 3, and 26.2% level 4 (from a 1995 base of 40% and 23% respectively). Various government initiatives - such as the learndirect helpline, learndirect centres and individual learning accounts - are intended to encourage more adults back into learning.

How to use this book

This book is designed to help you to find the course of study or training that is right for you. It also provides practical advice on how to cope with any difficulties you may encounter once you have made your choice. There are plenty of resources and agencies out there to help you.

Adult education centres, colleges, universities, learndirect centres and numerous independent education and training organisations offer ever-increasing opportunities for learning suitable for adults. Many of these are especially designed to fit around busy adult lives.

Introduction

If you find attending classes regularly difficult, or just off-putting, there are plenty of alternative ways to learn. Flexible, open and distance learning provision allows you to study at your own pace, in your own time, at work, at college or at home. So, whatever your reasons for returning to education or training, you should be able to find something to suit you.

If you need encouragement to come back to learning, take a look at the profiles we have included in this book. They describe the personal experiences of people who have taken the plunge. Some have sailed through their course of study or training with no problems, others have faced difficulties, but all are positive about the benefits they have accrued - whether social, work-related or academic. Improved self-confidence and self-image are often mentioned.

The profiles are:

- **Christina Palmer** - full-time Access course student - at the beginning of this introduction
- **Laurence Webb** - out of retirement into learning - chapter one
- **Rodd Budding** - gained an Open University Spanish Diploma - chapter one
- **Sarah Adams** - part-time Diploma of Higher Education student - chapter one
- **Alain Lewis** - an Open University undergraduate - chapter two
- **Janice Lawrence** - a 'return to learn' student - chapter three
- **Colin Brown** - following a full-time degree course - chapter three
- **Kevin Scott** - from no qualifications to certificates galore - chapter four
- **Adam Crosby** - gained several business-related qualifications whilst working as a civil servant - chapter four
- **Jean Ingham** - study for pleasure, and to become a volunteer literacy tutor - chapter four
- **Peter Walters** - came to terms with his PC - chapter four

- **Richard Griffiths** - gained employment through Work-based Learning for Adults - chapter five
- **Rebecca Malins** - full-time Access course student - chapter five
- **Siân Wiltshire** - part-time study while employed - chapter six
- **Ruth Farrow** - full-time higher education student - chapter seven
- **Sandra Small** - returning to teaching - chapter eight
- **Jacki Ciereszko** - accumulating IT qualifications while working - chapter nine.

Despite their satisfactory outcomes, many of the people featured in these profiles did have doubts and concerns before embarking on their courses. You should find answers to whatever doubts and concerns you may have within the chapters of this book.

- Need to justify your desire to learn? You'll find good reasons in chapter one.
- Not sure about current qualifications? See chapter four.
- What options are available? Chapters three and five will explain, and chapter seven will help you to choose.
- Worried about costs? Turn to chapter six.
- Don't know what to do with the kids? Try chapter eight.
- Where will it all lead? See chapter nine.

Within each chapter, you will find sources of further information on the topics covered.

Correcting some misconceptions

Despite the trend of more adults returning to education and training, there are still some misconceptions around.

'You can't teach an old dog new tricks'

Few adults drop out of study or training because they find it difficult to learn. On the contrary, college and university teachers and lecturers will tell you that adult learners are usually more motivated and more committed than their younger colleagues. Consequently they often do better.

Introduction

'I'm delighted to have proved to myself that I can study at this level ... it's a pleasure to use the brain to discuss, explore and argue about the things I want to.'

'Anyone is capable of achieving what they want, as long as they are committed.'

' ... the more I learn, the more I want to learn.'

'You can't get into higher education without A levels'

Entry into higher education is a lot more flexible than it used to be, even for school- and college-leavers. Where adult entrants are concerned, admissions tutors have always looked for evidence of ability to study to the required level, rather than specific academic qualifications. This is not because of a lowering of standards, but because they know that many people coming back to education, with no previous formal academic qualifications, have been successful students on all kinds of courses, including degrees.

'I had no qualifications other than a handful of O levels .... so I decided [successfully] to investigate the possibility of doing a degree in English literature ...'

'You'll be the only one there over 25'

Colleges and universities have always opened their doors to people of all ages. Many go out of their way to attract mature students, and current policies to widen access to education and training mean they are rewarded for doing so!

'... the mix of pupils [was] diverse, both sexes and a good range of ages. The diversity of people means you never feel that you stand out.'

'Having expected to be surrounded by spotty teenagers with raging hormones it was reassuring to be working with people my own age.'

'It won't help you to get a job'

Not only are employers demanding higher qualifications, but there are also increasingly strong links between education, training and industry. Many courses are directly work-related; some linked to particular employers. There are opportunities for gaining work experience on placements during courses, which sometimes leads to offers. National Vocational Qualifications place greater emphasis on practical ability, with assessment based on demonstrating competence and skill rather than passing theoretical exams.

> 'The qualifications have opened up career opportunities I'd never have had, enabled me to try different jobs and to earn more money.'

'It'll ruin your personal and family life'

A return to learning - especially full-time - can be difficult without the support of friends, partners and family. But many people find their lives and their relationships enriched by the experience.

> 'I now find that I am a calmer, more confident person than I ever was. My personal life has improved because of this. My children's attitude towards their own education has improved considerably; being a fellow student and a mother gives a fuller understanding of the teenage world!'

Do some networking

Talking to people who have been there before will quickly demolish many of the myths that surround education. In particular, they will tell you not to be easily discouraged and not to underestimate your abilities.

... and remember

> 'Study doesn't mean you have to give up all your spare time. You still have time to have fun!'

CHAPTER 1
Why learn?

Reasons, reasons

> *'it took the push of being unqualified and unemployed to give me the initial drive...'*
>
> *'to prove to myself that I am more than capable of ...'*
>
> *'more prosperous employment'*
>
> *'to gain in confidence'*
>
> *'retrain after redundancy'*
>
> *'you have to keep learning to keep your mind active'*
>
> *'to open doors'*
>
> *'my ambition to become a teacher seemed out of reach'*
>
> *'to access a more positive path'*
>
> *'to find an interest to focus on'*
>
> *'achieve a return to employment'*

If you invite a varied cross-section of adults to give their reasons for returning to learning, you will receive an equally varied range of responses. Each of the adults that you question will be able to produce an immediate, yet thoughtful, response. This is illustrated in the quotes given above, drawn from profiles contributed to this book by a range of adult learners. But then, of course, their reasons were very carefully considered before they took up their studies. Often, a decision to return to learning was only arrived at after lengthy deliberation and consultation, usually involving a wide range of people from amongst friends, family, colleagues, guidance professionals and tutors.

Of course, the responses to 'why learn?' are so varied because people take up learning from very different starting points. However, just like those adults quoted above, perhaps your reason for considering a return to learning can be allocated to one of these four slots:

➢ for interest and enjoyment
➢ to improve and, often, prove yourself
➢ to obtain qualifications that may raise your job and salary prospects
➢ to increase your work-readiness?

Who are the adult learners?

People from all walks of life take up learning again, often some time after leaving formal education. You may have a friend or know a colleague who goes to adult part-time study or leisure classes. And, you may be aware of someone who has recently retrained to take up a career that they had thought of, somewhat wishfully, over several years spent juggling home and family commitments with an unsatisfying job.

➢ Some learners were originally young entrants to the labour market who completed their formal education relatively recently and now want to improve their qualifications and job prospects.
➢ Many learners want to upgrade their level of basic skills in reading, writing and number work.
➢ Others are taking a pro-active approach to advancing their career through broadening their skills level and gaining additional qualifications.
➢ Many women, who held jobs without prospects and integral training before having a family, now need to re-skill and improve their employability.
➢ A large number have followed quite lengthy career paths and seek a change of direction – perhaps, more interesting and satisfying employment – for the middle stage of their working life and as they approach retirement.
➢ An equally large number of adult learners simply want to develop new interests.

CHAPTER 1 - Why learn?

When did we stop learning?

Considering the quite different reasons people give for returning to studying, probably, we would all agree that learning is not a stop-start activity. If we enjoy the challenge of a new situation – why do we cease to learn? Or, do we?

Of course not! It is simply that as we grow and adopt adult lifestyles and responsibilities, we tend to rely on established skills to function within our set routine. We often feel there is no time to study or follow pursuits that are not essential to doing our job adequately, or to supporting our friends and family. If we are coping well and with confidence, why return to learning?

We like to know

Everybody enjoys feeling that they are abreast of things – that they are up-to-date with the news, gossip or sport results, and are aware of popular books, films, music, TV programmes, travel ideas and life style choices. No-one likes to feel a stranger in their own culture. So how different is this familiarisation from learning? It is fun to be up-to-date with TV soaps and people may learn ways of handling their own life choices from considering the issues tackled in *Neighbours* or *Coronation Street*. And, we have terrific memories when it comes to remembering information highly significant to ourselves. Sports enthusiasts have very accurate recall of facts and figures connected with the teams they support; also, not many people forget their own birthday! It would seem that as we mature, we become highly selective in both the kind and amount of information that we are willing to take in.

So, what's in it for you?

If learning is the accumulation of knowledge and skills, we never opt out, although we can be quite unaware that the circumference of our knowledge is widening. Only gradually may it dawn on us that we have a fair grasp of a concept that we had not heard of a year or so ago. Think of the internet and shopping on-line! So, what are the reasons for taking up learning in a more pro-active way?

There are as many different reasons for taking up studying as there are people returning to learning. The profiles featured throughout the text are highly personal and emphasise the fact that everyone has a different start point from which they decide that learning is going to be a positive experience for them.

One, somewhat poignant, quote:

> 'With my children newly-independent, I found myself looking at my future and not liking what I saw...'

In the following sections, the broad reasons for coming back to learning –

> **fun and social engagement**
>
> **self-satisfaction and reward**
>
> **academic progress from any position – baseline to postgraduate**
>
> **to gain the vocational skills that employers seek**

– are explored in more detail.

Learning for fun and social reasons

Increasing your own knowledge about a subject or topic that interests you is fun, and the mental exercise can be rewarding in its own right. Your enjoyment of life can be given a boost through:

- using your spare time or leisure in a positive way
- brushing up your skills, or learning to do something rather better than before
- facing a new challenge – trying something that you have never done before
- adding to your pre-existing knowledge base
- finding out the unexpected.

There is an important social aspect to taking up learning. Whether learning is approached in a formal or informal way, it is usually pleasant, and can be great fun – to meet people with the same or similar interests. These interactions – based on a shared interest – can be supportive and help to improve your self-confidence and your ability to talk about aspects of your learning. You may widen your circle of friends.

> 'Another surprising aspect was how easy it was to get to know people – you're all there for the same reason and there was a

tendency to conduct group exercises, which forces you to mix with all the students at one time or another. The friendships you strike up were surprising too; some people from that first course (over ten years ago now) I still know!!!'

This social context of learning is usually strongest in settings where the learning is non-vocational and is approached through community education classes, residential leisure courses, summer schools, adult education offered by further education colleges or in the extra-mural classes run by higher education departments. Often, the learning content of leisure courses is tackled in an informal way, which can increase everyone's enjoyment by encouraging participation.

Laurence Webb – proving you're never too old!

I am a pensioner, not feeling resigned to sitting at home and stagnating. I applied and secured a job as a market research interviewer, which I did for a number of years. However, the organisation of my role changed and I did not see eye-to-eye with the new management, so I left.

Once again, I was left sitting at home with very little to do and I became bored. This is when I noticed an advertisement in the college prospectus; there were courses available on basic computing, so I lost no time in applying! My interest in computing had also been aroused by watching someone using a CD-ROM to demonstrate how wartime activities were carried out.

The first two or three weeks on the course seemed very difficult, and I despaired of ever mastering computing! Gradually, I started to make some sense of it, and it became easier. There were times when the computer seemed to have a vendetta against me! I must admit I got very frustrated, but there was a real sense of achievement when things started to come right. I then started to look forward to the next lesson, especially as we have a real dishy young female tutor!!!

I would strongly advise anyone finding themselves in the same situation to take advantage of any such opportunity as it restores your self-esteem.

Satisfaction is reward

There is satisfaction and pride to be derived from learning. Some of this satisfaction can be narrowed down to the fact that you gain in confidence through tackling something new, ambitious and demanding. Against all the odds – inexperience, lack of study skills, little time, no support, few funds – you make the effort and succeed, and can be justly proud of your achievement! Besides the satisfying knowledge that you have taken positive steps to reach a projected endpoint, and that you have done it voluntarily, without coercion, you may also benefit from:

- being able to make use of your new knowledge appropriately
- understanding and employing new technology
- having a wider, better-informed view on a subject and a broader base against which to assess new information
- improving your skills in interpreting information
- widening your vocational horizons and career prospects
- being able to trust your own abilities.

Some learning can give tangible benefits – think of re-creating excellent pastries in your own kitchen, the joy of playing an instrument or being able to re-upholster a favourite chair, or, of employing the most appropriate graph to display market research findings. Of course, if you collect new skills, you may gain qualifications, certificates to display – even prizes! But, whether or not your learning is validated with certificates, the life-enhancing benefits of having succeeded through your own efforts will emerge with time!

'The more you learn, the more confident you become.'

Academic improvement

Many people turn their thoughts to catching up on their general educational and basic skills levels only when they:

- need to find a job
- are planning to make a lifestyle change

CHAPTER 1 - Why learn?

> want to improve their prospects in work
> feel ready to make a career change.

Suddenly, it appears that 90% of job advertisements ask for basic computing skills, an ability with figures, clear communication and/ or experience in customer service work – many potential employers seeking people who can deal in a confident manner with clients and customers. It may be timely to look again at your levels of academic achievement, and to consider whether you might usefully upgrade your qualifications?

Basic skills

It is widely acknowledged that many people reach the end of their formal education still feeling unconfident about their reading and writing skills and their work with numbers. Low performance levels in basic skills may emerge only when people try to complete application forms in writing, search for jobs on-line or write speculative letters enquiring about work. Numerous people, from every kind of background, feel a need to improve their reading and comprehension skills, their grammar and spelling or, simply, their verbal construction and presentation skills. Many people who derived little benefit from their years in school decide, at a later date, to tackle and improve their low level of achievement in these basic skills. Some returners to learning want to be able to help their children achieve more from their schooling than they did themselves, and a feeling of ineffectiveness can challenge a parent's morale and provide the stimulus for self-improvement. Often, a renewed drive to learn arises from a need to find work.

Usually, only a small amount of dedicated time with an encouraging teacher is needed for people to overcome obstacles to learning, once they actively want to learn. Any earlier problems which may have presented difficulties – such as an unhappy or stressful learning environment – will have been largely overcome in adulthood. Individual cases – where a learner may need specialist help – can be identified, and different approaches tried to providing appropriate assistance.

General education

Many employers request 'a good general education' from job applicants, not necessarily specifying any particular subjects or grades. But, depending on the number and quality of applications for a vacancy, employers may prefer, nevertheless, to recruit from amongst those who have achieved a grade C or above in GCSE mathematics, English, and, possibly, science or a practically-based subject. IT skills also are usually a bonus as almost every job currently advertised involves the use of computers – if only at a basic level.

Rodd Budding – making good use of his time

'I take pleasure in having the opportunity to express how rewarding coming back to learning has been for me.

To start with I will reveal my unenviable circumstances. As a child, I probably held the record in each of the several schools I attended; sadly, not for my academic achievements but for the amount of mischief I managed to create. Perhaps it is not surprising that some years later I found myself in a small cell at Parkhurst Prison, perched on the Isle of Wight. In the same manner that an atheist may decide to turn to religion on impact with a crisis, I decided to escape to the Prison Education Department.

My principal aim was to improve my general English language and numeracy skills in order to better my employment chances after release. After quickly achieving that aim, I had developed an appetite to devour something more challenging. Having become friends with some Spanish-speaking students, I decided I wanted to learn their language. Fortunately, I had time on my side!

It has taken me four years to become fluent, working towards a Spanish Language Diploma with the Open University. I discovered that as a 30-year-old person I was far more capable of learning. With my targets in life better defined, my studies were tailored in a specific manner. Being able to choose my own subjects has injected enthusiasm and enjoyment. These are aspects that were absent during my childhood schooling.

Returning to learning has benefited me greatly. I now feel equipped to face the employment market of the outside world. Whilst my Spanish language studies were initially intended purely as a means of enjoyment, they have served in training me to study subsequent subjects in a methodical manner. Equally important, I must praise the dedication that teachers possess in terms of adult learning. I

CHAPTER 1 - Why learn?

have not once felt blamed for wasting my youth but often praised for striving to improve my future.

My advice to anyone considering coming back to learning is to also consider the following: How can the gaining of knowledge in a chosen subject of personal importance or enjoyment not enrich your life?

I hope my own story convinces you that, whatever your position in life may be, education can open a door that allows you access to a more positive path.'

Many adults return to learning to gain academic qualifications to satisfy entry requirements to careers training, or for entry to further or higher education courses. Also, the impetus can come from a desire to make progress in work, where further qualifications are often necessary to achieve a higher-grade position, or, to make a career change. Simply expressed by one mature learner:

> *'I realised that if I wanted a higher-grade job, I would need to be better qualified.'*

With a complete range of qualifications, accrediting every stage of academic progress, it is possible to amass quite an array of certificates! The level of qualifications sought for entry to many careers has risen over time. Today, few jobs are advertised for which employers seek low-level or no formal qualifications. Many recruiters want highly-skilled, motivated self-starters – flexible workers who work well either on their own initiative or in a team.

A degree more

An increasing number of careers actually demand degree-level qualifications, and adults lacking the formal qualifications for degree course entry are now encouraged to enter the academic field through preparative or access courses that also introduce ways to study and learn. Some professions require a specialised postgraduate qualification, before you can aspire to achieving full professional status.

If you have not felt motivated to raise your qualification levels on paper, you might reconsider your position in the light of an improvement of your financial prospects. There is plenty of accumulated evidence that degree holders who are in graduate employment – where there are high expectations of their levels of critical thinking and appraisal, information handling, powers of analysis, self-motivation etc – are paid at considerably higher rates than their employed peers who have not gained degree-equivalent qualifications. This pay differential widens with career progression, and the corollary is – graduates can look forward to a richer and, should they want it, earlier retirement!

Sarah Adams – digs in for a diploma

'All my life I've wanted to become a teacher and thought if I didn't take action now, my chance would have passed me by. I needed to study for three years at degree level, with a PGCE to complete my four years. After thought and discussion, the diploma was the best route for me. I have almost completed a year and a half of my diploma and, as yet, have never looked back. Without a doubt, the coursework was the most difficult aspect, with not having written an essay since being at school, (ten years ago) the whole thing seemed a daunting challenge. I guess it's a case of 'just trying' and see what happens!

In that first term, you do learn very much from your mistakes. This for me was a difficulty as I was unsure of what was expected at that time. Always being short of time is another dilemma as I also work and have a family, so trying to do all three is very demanding.

Of course there are benefits to being in education – such as you experience a whole new group of peers. It is a relief to speak to others, often in a similar situation to you, to talk over concerns and worries about the course. We do sometimes have fun in our lectures or on field trips, but above all, the greatest benefit is that you are actually learning.

Another specific thing which often gets on top of me is all the paper work – not merely the essays, but all the financial forms, leaflets and up-to-date information you have to keep track of. The best way is to 'just do it', then you don't give it time to build up. As far as essays are concerned, use all the help there is on offer – library, open learning centre and the teachers. They are there to help too and are paid to ensure you learn, so use them as a resource. (They've probably got all the good books you are looking for!)

Make sure to attend tutorials. They're not only a time when you can talk over concerns with the coursework, but also an opportunity to find out if you are receiving all possible financial help.

Don't get too strung up over your grades. Consider various methods of writing your assignments, and if one way is not approved then channel another route. Experiment, until you find a way that suits you.

My advice to anybody returning to study would be to keep focused on what's ahead. It's so easy to get bogged down with what today holds; it's a case of looking beyond and striving for your end achievement. Remember what incentive brought you to college originally and why you chose to return. In my case, I returned to become a qualified teacher. Some of the subjects I am covering seem somewhat irrelevant to teaching six year-olds; although I cannot deny there is self-satisfaction in expanding my own education!'

Rarified learning

Of course, some people simply love to learn! With this self-improving approach to study, the acquisition of knowledge becomes all-important and the learning can be quite esoteric – perhaps, only shared with a select few. This kind of learning we often talk of as 'learning for learning's sake' – the purpose of which can be to gain an informed view or opinion, or to encourage philosophical reflection – really, to become wiser.

Vocational learning

With the present emphasis on people raising their skills levels, there has been a push from the Government to encourage everybody to take their learning to as high a level as possible. The concept of lifelong learning has now taken hold across the work culture, and is actively promoted for the retired and semi-retired.

Certainly, there have never been so many opportunities to gain skills and qualifications in the workplace. Many adults who fight shy of entering formal educational institutions find that they can happily accumulate evidence for accreditation of their skills in performing tasks in the workplace – and so gain nationally-recognised vocational qualifications. These credits are transferable between occupational areas and may be awarded for prior acquisition of knowledge and skills in earlier employment or learning.

Young adults can take up employment with training in the workplace. Through this route, they are able to match the level of qualification gained by learners following full-time vocational courses in further education colleges (all of which are open to adults). The added bonus of work-based training is that, in many cases, you are employed by the company you are training with and, comparatively, acquire far more experience of the actual work.

Further education courses, combined with the range of distance or open learning options made available through multimedia, create a vast array of vocational learning opportunities! If you are interested in taking a course to ease your entry to employment, then almost anything is possible. You will have to pick your way carefully, and may well need guidance in interpreting which courses are most appropriate for increasing your employability.

If you have been in employment for some time, you may be offered the opportunity to further your occupational skills through in-house training, being sent on training courses by your employer, or through broadening your abilities with distance learning courses. Larger and expanding companies are more likely to have a pro-active policy regarding employee training and lifelong learning, being keen to encourage a highly-skilled and motivated workforce.

Vocational courses all have a large practical element and can help you:

- prepare for entry to the world of work
- build up your key skills
- update your skills, or re-skill, to gain the capabilities that employers seek today
- prepare for voluntary work
- build subject interests into occupational strengths
- improve your job skills and level of working
- help you acquire the business skills essential for self-employment
- work towards a supervisory/management-level qualification
- train to a highly-skilled level in a specific craft
- accumulate credits for your skills in using IT as a tool.

However, don't feel that all your learning has to enhance your employability. Although position and salary are important, they are not everything in life, and remember, there is life after work!

Further information

How To Books publish a range called Career Development Texts which include:

Building Your Life Skills – a personal action plan – by Judith Johnstone, £12.95

Planning a New Career – by Judith Johnstone, £9.99

Learning New Job Skills – by Laurel Alexander, £9.99

Enhancing Your Employability – by Roderic Ashley, £9.99

Survive Redundancy and Thrive – by Laurel Alexander, £9.99

Employability – how to get your career on the right track (£12.99) and *Creating Your Career – practical advice for graduates in a changing world* (£8.99) – both published by Kogan Page.

Coming Back to Learning

CHAPTER 2
Sources of advice and guidance

If you've made your mind up to return to learning, you will need reliable information and advice before taking your next step. If you still haven't decided if a return to education or training is for you, or you are unsure of the learning route you want to take, you may need professional guidance. Some sources of help are described below, under the following headings:

- course providers
- educational and careers guidance agencies for adults
- Training and Enterprise Councils (Learning and Skills Councils from April 2001) and Local Enterprise Companies
- Jobcentres
- voluntary agencies, campaigns and charities
- professional bodies.

Organisations covered by the first four headings are primarily local sources of help, providing a service to a particular region or catchment area – although with national links. Under the last two headings, you will find organisations that offer a service for specific groups of people, or that can provide information about particular careers and industries. So, for example, in the section on voluntary agencies there are details of agencies that can advise women, older people, people with disabilities, ex-offenders and refugees, while the professional bodies cater for would-be engineers, teachers, social workers etc.

Alain Lewis - took his own advice

'When I left school, in the dim and distant past, I felt satisfied with the two O levels I'd gained at grade C in English and maths. As the years passed, though, I began to realise that I could have done better than this. This state of mind was reinforced by contact with lots of people who were better qualified, but not cleverer, than me. This was in 1987 after I had done a succession of low-grade temporary jobs. I came to the realisation that, if I wanted a higher-grade job, I would need to be better qualified.

I began by studying for GCSEs, passing history and art. After a few false starts and wrong turns, including starting (and not finishing) a BTEC National in Graphic Design, I came to the position I'm in now. I'm studying for an Open University history degree while working as an advisor for a Lifelong Learning Partnership. I'm delighted to have proved to myself that I can study at this level -although it is difficult to do a full day's work and then come home to read about pre-World War I German naval policy. It's a pleasure to use the brain to discuss, explore and argue about the things I want to.

Being an undergraduate, I have gained more confidence about my prospects and where I might end up. I feel better able to analyse, reflect and act - assessing situations rather than taking lots of chances. Studying with the OU has enabled me to meet lots of interesting and different people on the variety of courses I've done, and at the summer school I've attended. It's well worthwhile studying as an adult, and it's even more worthwhile doing some research before embarking on a course. Find out what is involved in doing a course and what you might expect to gain from it. You may also need to check whether this matches your expectations, working out whether it's worth giving time to a particular course. Seek advice and guidance if you need it.

I'm very happy with the progress I've made, and I know that I wouldn't have got here if I hadn't taken the plunge all those years ago. So come on in; the water's lovely!'

The course providers

Chapter 2 - Sources of advice and guidance

Just as students have a story to tell, so do the people who work in education and training centres, colleges and universities. Staff will be able to tell you in detail about the courses they run, what might be suitable for you and how previous people on the course have fared. Much information will be available on their website and in the prospectus, but there are usually questions to which you will want a more personalised answer.

Many adult education centres, colleges and universities are able to provide general educational guidance as well as giving detailed information about the courses they offer. For the most part these services are designed for potential students, but some colleges also provide information about courses offered by other learning providers in their locality.

As well as information about their courses, colleges are well placed to advise on issues such as fees, access funds and childcare. They can tell you about entry requirements and how you can get credit for your current skills through assessment of your previous learning and experience (APL and APEL).

Try to talk to the right person. While the reception and enquiry desks will be able to deal with many general enquiries, you will need to speak to other staff to get detailed advice and guidance. Ask if the college has anyone who specialises with enquiries and applications from mature students. Otherwise, try the admissions staff, student services unit or advice and guidance centre (or any permutation of these – titles vary). If you are interested in a particular course, ask to speak to one of the course tutors.

> 'I discussed the workload with the admissions tutor, who gave me information on the amount of private study required. This enabled me to make an informed decision. I also spoke to the university careers adviser before making my course choice'.

> 'My advice to anyone contemplating enrolling on a course is to find out as much as possible about the course before you commit yourself.... Time taken at this stage will help to eliminate the possibility of a bad experience!'

If you have a specific occupational area in mind, but are having difficulty finding a training provider, you can contact that industry's National Training Organisation (NTO). The NTO National Council can put you in touch with the appropriate body.

NTO National Council – 10 Meadowcourt, Amos Road, Sheffield S9 1BX. Tel: 0114 261 9926.

Cyngor NTO Cymru – Suite 17, Technocentre, Beignon Close, Ocean Way, Cardiff CF24 5PB. Tel: 029 2046 0776.

You'll also find details on website: www.nto-nc.org

Educational and careers guidance services for adults

The quickest way to find out what educational and careers guidance services for adults are available in your area is to ring the learndirect helpline on 0800 100 900.

At present, services to adults vary considerably from one area to another. What you get for free, and what you have to pay for, depends on the local service's policy. With the advent of Learning and Skills Councils and other changes to existing systems, the Department for Education and Employment is providing a national framework and specifications for local information, advice and guidance (IAG) services to adults. The network of services on offer in your area will be coordinated through an IAG partnership and will have to meet national quality standards. The service may be provided through various channels in the public, private and voluntary sectors. For the year 2000-2001, Government funding only covers the provision of information and advice; professional individual guidance is most likely to be provided as an extra priced service – although disadvantaged groups may be eligible for free guidance.

Guidance services should be impartial, confidential and independent. That means they are not tied to recommending any particular educational institution, training provider or course of action.

Each IAG provider should have information about the range of educational and training opportunities available in their locality, including basic skills provision. In addition, advisers are available (often by appointment only) to help you make sense of the options – although detailed individual guidance, as stated earlier – may only be available at a price. Information and advice are available on study fees and other costs, and about the availability of financial support. Some centres offer computer-assisted careers guidance, psychometric testing, and careers counselling. Adult guidance services will have links with careers services for young people; some may share premises. In any case, adults are able to use the information

Chapter 2 - Sources of advice and guidance

in careers service careers libraries as well as in agencies specifically for adults.

Likely to be available for reference are information from professional bodies and others, college and university prospectuses and directories and databases, such as:

The Directory of Further Education – published by CRAC

University and College Entrance: the official guide – published by UCAS

Occupations – published by COIC (which includes a paragraph on late entry to many careers)

What do Graduates Do? – information on graduate destinations published by AGCAS

TAP - a localised database of training opportunities

ECCTIS UK Course Discover – a database of further and higher education courses UK-wide.

A useful list of UK-wide contacts, divided into geographical areas, can be found in the Gazetteer section of the DfEE publication – *Second Chances* – which should be available for reference in careers centres, and can also be viewed on the Internet: www.dfee.gov.uk/secondchances

Information on courses and funding and issues such as childcare is available on the learndirect helpline: 0800 100 900. The learndirect website offers information about courses available at learndirect centres: www.learndirect.co.uk

There are a number of private careers and educational guidance consultancies, which charge fees for advice and guidance. Some are very reputable and offer a comprehensive service. Check whether what they offer could not be obtained cheaper – or even for free – from the Government-funded service, and that their staff are suitably qualified to give guidance and to supervise psychometric tests etc.

In **Northern Ireland**, information is available from your regional Education and Library Boards and Training and Employment Agency offices, or directly from:

The Educational Guidance Service for Adults (EGSA) – 4th Floor, Linenhall Street, Belfast BT2 8BA. Tel: 028 9024 4274. Website: www.egsa.org.uk

Scotland has 17 regional adult guidance networks, which vary considerably in what they offer, as well as provision through local careers services and adult guidance services. The Scottish Executive, which funds the networks, is currently looking at all-age careers guidance provision - so watch this space! As in England and Wales, the learndirect helpline on 0800 100 900 can put you in touch with your nearest guidance network or education and training provider.

Training and Enterprise Councils (Learning and Skills Councils from April 2001) and Local Enterprise Companies

Set up in 1989, TECs in England and Wales and LECs in Scotland have been involved in educational and careers guidance and training initiatives as part of their wider remit to support economic development, working with both local and national government. (In some areas of England and Wales, TECs are known as Chambers of Commerce, Training and Enterprise or CCTEs.) The role of the new Learning and Skills Councils will be more closely linked to further education and training provision and funding, and to adult information and guidance. LECs will continue much as they are now.

Each TEC has had considerable scope to decide its own priorities, therefore provision has varied considerably in different localities. Your local TEC can tell you about training opportunities in your area.

In Northern Ireland all training schemes and related initiatives are run by the Training and Employment Agency.

Look in the telephone directory or contact your local Jobcentre for details about the TECs/LECs/LSCs in your area.

Jobcentres

Although primarily a job-finding agency, your local Jobcentre will also have printed information and computer databases on education and training opportunities for job-changers. More specifically, it is your major point of contact for information about government-funded training schemes. In some areas, Jobcentres and Benefits Agency offices share premises so you can find answers to all your queries in the one place.

Voluntary agencies, campaigns and

Chapter 2 - Sources of advice and guidance

charities

Many voluntary agencies and charities are concerned with education and training. In many cases, this concern takes the form of campaigning for better access for particular groups in society. But some agencies are a useful source of additional information and can provide specialist educational guidance and counselling - and sometimes even training provision. Listed here are additional sources of help for women, older people, people with disabilities, ex-offenders, refugees and overseas students.

For women

Campaigns to promote better opportunities for women in education and training operate both at a national and a local level. They can be useful sources of information about education provision. A few organisations with a national profile are described here.

The Women Returners' Network – WRN, Chelmsford College, Moulsham Street, Chelmsford, Essex CM2 0JQ. Tel: 01245 263796. Website: www.womenreturners.org.uk

This organisation works for greater education, training and employment opportunities to help women re-enter the workforce. The network encourages providers of education to develop flexible education and training programmes to meet the needs of women. At the time of writing, WRN is updating *Returning to Work: a national directory of training and information for women returners*, which will be available both as a priced publication and on their website.

Women into Science and Engineering (WISE) - 2 Queen Anne's Gate Buildings, Dartmouth Street, London SW1H 9BP. Tel: 020 7227 8421. Website: www.wisecampaign.org

WISE is a campaign to encourage more girls and women to consider careers in science and engineering. The Women's Engineering Society is at the same address. Launched in 1984 by the Engineering Council and the Equal Opportunities Commission, WISE publishes an annual free directory– entitled *Directory of Initiatives* – listing information on awards, scholarships, courses and family-friendly policies. There is also a *Directory of Scottish Initiatives*.

During the 1990s, WISE initiatives have been set up in Northern Ireland, Wales and Scotland.

WISE in Northern Ireland – c/o Dr Deirdre Griffith, Industrial Research and Technology Unit, 17 Antrim Road, Lisburn BT28 3AL. Tel: 028 9262 3161.

WISE in Wales – c/o Dr C J Moore, Cardiff School of Engineering, Cardiff University, PO Box 686, Cardiff CF24 3TB. Tel: 029 2087 4000.

WISE in Scotland – c/o Jo Beswick, Department of Physics and Applied Physics, University of Strathclyde, John Anderson Building, 107 Rottenrow, Glasgow G4 0NG. Tel: 0141 548 4826.

Women's Training Network – Northway Centre, Maltfield Road, Marston, Oxford OX3 9RF. Tel: 01865 741317.

A national non-profit making organisation which promotes vocational training for disadvantaged women in areas of work where women are under-represented – such as construction, IT, electronics etc.

For older learners

The guidance services and most further and higher education programmes featured throughout this book are generally available to anyone regardless of age. However, much purely vocational training will have an upper age limit – even if it is sometimes as high as 60. But most education institutions work on the principle that it is never too late to learn, and educational guidance services should be able to offer good advice to people of all ages. The following are organisations that cater specifically for older people.

NIACE: The National Organisation for Adult Learning – The Older and Bolder Programme Information Officer, 21 De Montfort Street, Leicester LE1 7GE. Tel: 0116 204 4227. Website: www.niace.org.uk

NIACE works for all adults, but its Older and Bolder programme specifically promotes learning opportunities for people over 50. If you think that's over the hill, the national winners of the Oldest and Most Inspiring Learner awards for the year 2000 were aged 107 and 94 respectively. Regional award winners (the youngest being in their 80s) are learning everything from ancient Greek to Tai Chi. *'Anything that is not used goes rusty, and that includes the brain'* – says 90-year-old computing student, Mrs May Machell!

Age Concern – Freepost (SWB 30375), Ashburton, Devon TQ13 7ZZ or freephone 0800 00 99 66 to obtain a factsheet entitled Leisure and Learning. Website: www.ace.org.uk

Chapter 2 - Sources of advice and guidance

Age Concern collects information on education and leisure activities for older people. As the first point of contact, get in touch with Age Concern locally. There are some 1400 groups and organisations throughout the country. They should be able to advise you about local opportunities or point you in the right direction.

The University of the Third Age (U3A) – National Office, 26 Harrison Street, London WC1H 8JG. Tel: 020 7837 8838. Website: www.u3a.org.uk

U3A provides an opportunity for older people to share educational, creative and leisure activities. The idea behind the University is to bring education further into the community, providing more opportunities for all older people, not simply to learn but also to teach and share their knowledge and experience with others. Because of this informal style of learning, no qualifications are involved. The University now has around 85,000 members in over 400 local groups. Write (with s.a.e.) or email to national.office@u3a.org.uk for details of local groups.

Third Age Employment Network – St James's Walk, Clerkenwell Green, London EC1R 0BE. Tel: 020 7242 6273. Website: www.taen.co.uk

Through local groups, this organisation pools information on guidance and training as well as employment issues.

For people with disabilities

There are a number of organisations that can provide specialist advice for people with disabilities. Before consulting them, it is worth talking to the educational guidance agencies who may be well informed both about opportunities and about how people with disabilities have fared previously with local education providers. Colleges, adult education centres and universities may be able to help directly. Most have appointed staff with responsibility for co-ordinating support for disabled people. As a requirement of the Disability Discrimination Act, colleges and universities must, at least, be able to tell you about their facilities and services for students with disabilities. The Act is being closely monitored, and further requirements for students are likely to be incorporated in the future. Many providers already go further than the minimum requirement: they will be able to advise on course options, help with transport and access and arrange support for those with particular learning difficulties. The Open University has a specialist adviser for students with disabilities, and a team of volunteers who assist students with disabilities at summer schools.

Disability Discrimination Act Information – Freepost M1D02 164, Stratford-upon-Avon CV37 9BR. Can provide a catalogue of publications relevant to the DDA in print, Braille or audio versions.

Skill (the National Bureau for Students with Disabilities) – Chapter House, 18-20 Crucifix Lane, London SE1 3JW. Tel: 020 7450 0620. Website: www.skill.org.uk

Skill campaigns to increase opportunities in education, training and employment for people with disabilities or learning difficulties. The Bureau is concerned with people whose needs arise from physical and sensory disabilities, learning difficulties or mental health problems.

Skill operates an information service, which welcomes enquiries by letter or by telephone, and publishes a number of useful information sheets for those wishing to return to education.

RNIB Education and Employment Information Service – RNIB, 224 Great Portland Street, London W1N 6AA. Tel: 020 7388 1266. Website: www.rnib.org.uk

RNIB Vocational College – Radmoor Road, Loughborough, Leicestershire LE11 3BS. Tel: 01509 611077.

The Royal National Institute for the Blind (RNIB) has a student support service for those in (or planning to be in) further and higher education. RNIB advisers can provide guidance on finance and courses, including provision at RNIB specialist colleges for people with visual impairment. They can advise on the range of specialist equipment available to facilitate study. There are a number of RNIB residential specialist colleges throughout the UK, one of these being the RNIB Vocational College in Loughborough. Students can study a broad range of courses, from specialist vocational courses to courses offered in partnership with Loughborough College, such as NVQs, GNVQs, HNDs and academic and vocational A levels.

RADAR – Unit 12, City Forum, 250 City Road, London EC1V 8AF. Tel: 020 7250 3222. Website: www.radar.org.uk

The Royal Association for Disability and Rehabilitation (RADAR) works for people with disabilities on a range of issues. Organised into local groups – including, of course, disabled people – one of

Chapter 2 - Sources of advice and guidance

RADAR's aims is to help people with disabilities make informed choices about education.

For ex-offenders

NACRO – 169 Clapham Road, London SW9 0PU. Tel: 020 7582 6500. Website: www.nacro.org.uk

Established in 1966, NACRO is the leading charity working to promote social inclusion, reduce crime and resettle offenders. NACRO runs practical projects for offenders, ex-offenders and other vulnerable people across England and Wales. These include training and employment projects for people in contact with the Criminal Justice System - both in prisons and in the community. The focus of much of this work is on enabling people to gain both vocational and basic skills, such as literacy and communication, in order to live constructive and law-abiding lives.

NACRO also works to inform policy, including in the areas of offender employment and special needs education and training.

SACRO – 1 Broughton Market, Edinburgh EH3 6NU. Website: www.sacro.org.uk

In Scotland there are no comparable educational guidance services for ex-offenders, although SACRO can help in other matters.

NIACRO – 169 Ormeau Road, Belfast BT7 1SQ. Tel: 028 9032 0157.

Although they do not have a dedicated education service, the Northern Ireland Association for the Care and Resettlement of Offenders (NIACRO) can provide information and advice on education matters. NIACRO also runs training programmes in conjunction with the New Deal and other schemes.

For non-UK nationals

For those from overseas, the main educational and careers guidance services are useful sources of information. Colleges and community education centres are also helpful. Many run ESOL courses (English for speakers of other languages), some in conjunction with educational guidance and careers counselling. In addition to the main guidance agencies, other organisations which offer specialist guidance to refugees and others from overseas are:

Coming Back to Learning

World University Service Refugee Education and Training Advisory Service (RETAS) – 14 Dufferin Street, London EC1Y 8PD. Tel: 020 7426 5800.

RETAS has information on all aspects of the UK educational system, and can advise on professional requalification and on eligibility to student support and other benefits. The service also offers some specialised training schemes of its own for refugees, such as business start-up and jobsearch courses and NVQ level 3 in advice and guidance.

The Refugee Council – 3-9 Bondway House, London SW8 1SJ. Tel: 020 7820 3000. Website: www.refugeecouncil.org.uk

The Council has an education and training centre, and helps refugees and asylum seekers to obtain accreditation of their overseas qualifications as well as offering assistance in obtaining education and training in the UK.

The UK NARIC – ECCTIS 2000 Ltd, Oriel House, Oriel Road, Cheltenham GL50 1XP. Tel: 01242 260010. Website: www.naric.org.uk

The UK NARIC (National Academic Recognition Information Centre) helps people to relate their overseas academic qualifications to the British system. The service is free to individuals - unless exceptionally lengthy research is required. A certificate of comparability costs £25. Write, enclosing a photocopy of your certificate, with translation if necessary, or fax a copy to 01242 258611.

Professional bodies

There are numerous organisations that can provide careers advice and educational guidance related to specific trades, vocations and professions. These range from professional associations such as the Royal Institute of British Architects to bodies with a responsibility for recruitment such as the Teacher Training Agency. These organisations should at least be able to give general information about the type of qualifications you will need for entry into a particular career at a given point. At best, they might be able to offer more comprehensive advice on prospects, on courses (including those which give exemption to professional exams) and

Chapter 2 - Sources of advice and guidance

on which colleges and universities have good reputations in the relevant disciplines. Most have websites as well as printed information.

For anybody considering education as a route into a particular career, it is worth trying to find out if there is an appropriate professional body or organisation which covers the profession. For example, if you wish to study to become a photographer and want advice on appropriate courses, then try contacting the British Institute of Professional Photography. Unfortunately, there is no easy way of finding out which organisations can advise about particular careers; arrangements vary from profession to profession. However, the educational and careers guidance services featured earlier in the chapter should be able to help. You can use careers centre libraries to find addresses. Staff will show you how to make sense of the classification system! *Occupations* – published by COIC and in all careers centres – is a good starting point.

Other sources of information

Local reference libraries will have books and databases on local and national education and training opportunities. Your Citizens' Advice Bureau can help you on issues such as entitlement to benefits while studying. 'Quality' newspapers often carry articles about careers, labour market and education issues – watch out for those buzzwords 'lifelong learning'!

Coming Back to Learning

CHAPTER 3
Ways to learn

Chapter one looked at the reasons why people return to learning; in this chapter, the emphasis is on the merits of different ways of studying. In recent years, the opportunities for adults wanting to return to learning have increased greatly. This is due in part to a much more flexible approach by colleges and universities.

- There is greater scope to study for all types of qualifications on a part-time basis or through open learning.
- It is easier to transfer between courses.
- It is becoming more common to be able to get accepted to courses on the basis of a much wider range of previous learning and work experience than just academic qualifications.

There is a wide choice of what you can study, how you study and where you can study.

When you are trying to decide on the right course for you, a practical consideration will concern the way the course is organised. This will have a large bearing on whether it can be successfully combined with your current work and domestic responsibilities.

Make sure you find a course that suits your personal circumstances.

You can study full-time, part-time, day release, evening, on short courses or in seminars, or by flexible and open learning. Education providers increasingly recognise that flexibility is important for adults. The best institutions make efforts to structure courses accordingly. For instance, they may run programmes at evenings and weekends or on a part-time basis, or schedule classes so that parents can take and collect children to and from school.

Look for establishments which offer you the flexibility in how and when you study.

Full-time study

Returning to full-time study requires making sacrifices but, as many mature students report, it can be enormously satisfying. There are definite advantages, not least that by making the commitment to a full-time course you may be more able to make the most of education, benefiting from regular contact and support from tutors and fellow students and using educational facilities to the full. Additionally, full-time study usually offers the quickest route to qualifications.

It can be tough financially. You may have to pay the full cost of the course; you may be asked to contribute towards tuition fees. You may be eligible for student loans. Full information about financial matters is given in chapter six.

Full-time does not necessarily mean nine-to-five attendance, five days a week. In higher education, (post A level and the equivalent) most courses at colleges and universities involve substantial amounts of independent study and learning; lectures, tutorials and workshops may account for as little as half the week. The academic year only occupies between 30 and 33 weeks of the year, so there is time to attend to the rest of your life. Indeed, some students manage to combine part-time or shift work with a full-time course, although for many this is through economic necessity rather than choice. But, in general, it can be difficult to juggle other responsibilities. Your family may have to make sacrifices as well – certainly, you will need to find time to study – so it is very important at the outset to get their backing and support. For strategies on coping successfully, see chapter eight.

Chapter 3 - Ways to learn

Studying part-time

The obvious advantage of part-time study is that it is easier to combine study with work and domestic responsibilities. You have the opportunity to study for much the same set of qualifications without making the rather greater commitment demanded by full-time education. The down side is that it usually takes longer to obtain qualifications.

The term 'part-time' covers a multitude of arrangements. These include:

- day release – attendance one day a week
- shortened day – classes from 10 am to 3 pm for parents with school-age children
- day/evening combined – perhaps one afternoon and one evening a week
- evening classes.

These are all taught courses. Part-time study can also be through flexible learning.

There is perhaps greatest choice for studying for GCSEs and A levels. Leisure and recreational courses are typically run in the evening or during a shortened day. Many part-time higher education courses will require some attendance during the day, although a growing number are being offered on an evening-only basis.

Janice Lawrence - decided on a Return to Learn course

'The need to return to employment after years of full-time parenting was creeping ever closer, and the prospects of achieving this was quite daunting. The opportunity to learn new skills and improve my standard of education was what I was looking for, and to achieve this, I would have to gain qualifications. I decided to take the plunge and return to learning to allow me to fulfil this goal.

Being out of the education system for so long was a worrying aspect for me. Having lost confidence and being computer-illiterate was not helping the situation. I decided to enrol on a short course. 'Return to Learn' looked to be the ideal course for me. A 10-week course, one session a week, which gave the option of improving

43

> basic skills in English and/or computing, was just what I was looking for.
>
> Being honest, I put off this moment on numerous occasions. This probably sounds ridiculous, but it took a lot of courage to take this first step and even a few sleepless nights. Having taken the plunge, I haven't looked back. The support and encouragement given on this course helped to build my confidence. Having completed this course, I went on to 'First Steps Back to Work' and passed CLAIT 1 in IT. I have just finished 'Effective Business Writing' and have enrolled on the 'Microsoft Office for Improvers'.
>
> The benefits for me personally have been enormous, and in the future I feel I will benefit both in job satisfaction and financially.
>
> My advice to anyone contemplating enrolling on a course is to find out as much as possible about the course before you commit yourself. Consider the amount of homework required, any cost you might incur, or most importantly, is this course for you? Time taken at this stage will help to eliminate the possibility of a bad experience! Don't take on anything you feel you're going to struggle with, set yourself goals, be positive and you will enjoy the experience.
>
> If time is on your side, invest it wisely and enrol on one of the short part-time courses available, some of which are free. This way, you're not committed to anything long term and the rewards are instant, giving you a sense of achievement and, in some cases, credit in the form of a recognised certificate.'

Modular courses

Many courses are now organised on a modular basis – divided up into many parts – allowing you to build up course by course towards a qualification, and giving you many more options about what, how and when you study. Each of these 'mini courses' covers a particular aspect of a course. You could build up your modules, at a pace to suit yourself.

Many higher education courses are offered on a modular basis, where the course content has been divided into a number of separate units, but all relate to a specific degree. Some of the units are compulsory, some are optional. Degrees are awarded when the necessary number of units has been obtained. This type of study is especially attractive to people with other commitments.

Each module has a specific credit rating. Students may build up credit towards a degree by successfully completing individual modules. Then, if a student wishes or has to change courses, move to another institution or take a break from study, the Credit Accumulation and Transfer Scheme (CATS) allows the retention and transfer of credit for the modules that have already been passed. More about this in chapter four.

It is, for example, now even possible to study, for some Master's degree programmes on a modular basis.

Short courses

Short courses can be full-time or part-time. In some ways, short courses combine some of the advantages of full-time and part-time study.

> You can pack a great deal of learning into an intensive short course.

> You may find a spell of concentrated study on a two-week course preferable to studying on a day-release basis over 10 or more weeks.

> You can take courses as and when you need to learn.

> They do not require the commitment demanded by longer courses.

For these reasons, short courses have been favoured by many employers as a means of training staff.

Universities, consultancies and private training companies compete vigorously for the short-course market in areas such as marketing, computing, management training and languages. They offer courses to suit both individual students and business clients. These range from one-day seminars and workshops, weekend schools through to one-week or two-week programmes run on a day attendance or residential basis.

Short part-time courses, particularly those for women returners, are a very effective way of developing new skills and restoring confidence.

Colin Brown – from part-time study whilst working to a full-time degree

'Leaving school with eight CSEs was, I felt, sufficient to start working life. Over a number of years I worked up to skilled machinist in the aircraft industry. However, as my training was not indentured I did not have any formal qualifications to 'prove' my training. When the site I worked at faced closure, we were interviewed by other sites within the company with the aim of relocating. Some personnel managers were openly disdainful of a person with my lack of qualifications and offered only menial work with no prospect of advancement.

The experience left a deep impression on me and I was determined to change my level of qualifications. I enrolled at the local college for a BTEC National Certificate in mechanical production engineering. The course supervisor suggested that I took a one-year First Certificate course before the National. This was well founded advice as it enabled me to get used to study on a course which was not academically challenging; in retrospect, confidence building from the first steps was all important to help overcome doubts and anxieties over my abilities.

After successfully completing the First Certificate my employers were favourable in sponsoring me for the National Certificate; they continued their support through to HND. This led to increased involvement at work, which substantially improved my job satisfaction.

Since then I have been able to enrol at university full-time to study mechanical engineering. This is a different approach to study compared to day release; I found it a bit of a shock to find how quickly the course moved. In deciding whether I could undertake the demands of a degree, I discussed the workload with the admissions tutor who gave information on the amount of private study required. This enabled me to make an informed decision. I also spoke to the university careers adviser before making my course choice.

It has taken a little time to get used to the demands of a degree and coping as a single parent, but it is all very fulfilling. It is important to discuss the demands of the course with tutors, and to decide what is wanted from the course. Now being forty, I would have liked to have returned to study a lot earlier. It took the 'push'

Chapter 3 - Ways to learn

of being unqualified to give me the initial drive. There is no need to wait to be pushed when it's just as easy to take the plunge.'

Distance, open and independent learning

Open learning (or flexible learning as it is often called) is, in many ways, an attractive option in that it allows you to study in your own time and at your own pace. You can organise study periods around your other commitments using prepared learning materials. Typically, these consist of private study textbooks, exercises and assignments to check your progress and understanding, background reading material and, perhaps, video and audio cassettes; there are also a number of interactive computer-based systems. Courses are available at all levels, from basic to postgraduate.

Many universities are trying to make higher education more accessible for adults. Some have formal arrangements with colleges of further education, which allow you to take a pre-degree foundation year and the first year of the degree itself at a local college. Others are exploring ways of linking into widely scattered communities through the use of flexible and distance learning, supported by outstations, modern communications technology and learning centres and, perhaps, local colleges. These approaches, combined with some commuting on a part-time basis to the university, may provide additional opportunities to study for a degree.

Given the advantages, it is perhaps no surprise that open learning is regarded as the training and education mode of the future. However, some people might find there are drawbacks.

- ➢ The unstructured nature of open learning can itself turn out to be a disadvantage.
- ➢ If you are not self-disciplined it is easy to drop courses as other pressures or interests arise.
- ➢ It can be isolating, you can miss the stimulus of fellow students, and you can miss out on the support and encouragement of tutors.

This is why simple teach yourself packages are rarely entirely effective. To be successful as a learning medium, flexible learning packages need:

- good support and backup from tutors
- a unit or assignment structure to encourage learners to progress step by step
- opportunities to work with other students in workshops, tutorials or summer schools
- a range of different learning materials with practical exercises.

In practice, you have two options.

Distance learning

You can choose to study at home, enrolling on a course offered by a distance learning organisation. The best courses provide you with learning materials and self-study packs, tutorial support and a system for assessing and marking your assignments. Leaders in distance education include the Open University, the Open College of the Arts and the National Extension College.

Distance education is clearly suitable for those who live a long way from the nearest college or university, and the success of the Open University shows that this option has widespread appeal. There is more about this in chapter five.

Open learning

Open learning allows you to study at a time to suit yourself, independently, using specially-written materials, but with tutor support. You can learn through flexible learning packages, usually using a computer, at local open learning centres and colleges. Where these are available, there will be tutors on hand to guide you through the materials and to help you with any problems. Many colleges are setting up open learning centres and investing in modern interactive educational technology. These centres offer you the chance to arrange a customised study programme for your maximum convenience. Tutor-assisted independent learning allows you to study at a pace that you negotiate with your tutor; you could study at home or in the college and attend tutorials on a regular basis. Some centres have 'drop-in' arrangements; you can use them as and when you can find the time to attend. Staff are able to advise you on the best courses to meet your particular needs and to help you overcome difficulties.

Chapter 3 - Ways to learn

Launched in November 1999, UfI learndirect centres – the government-backed network of learndirect centres across the UK – are part of the drive for lifelong learning. This is a new venture, which will eventually see centres opened in sites as varied as shopping centres, pubs, doctors' surgeries, football clubs, colleges and libraries. They are run by employers, voluntary organisations, training providers, colleges and universities. At present, they focus on IT skills, business and management skills, multimedia etc. Most of the learning materials are computer-based; print and broadcast media will also be used.

Other independent learning

There are different ways to learn which you can do independently, without the benefit of any tutorial support – through books, tapes, videos, TV and computer programs. This is perhaps a more difficult route, as you do not have any specialist advice and support, but it is a good way to learn if travelling to a learning centre is a problem, or the time you can devote to study is limited.

- There are plenty of teach-yourself books, computer handbooks etc on the market.
- Tapes and CDs are a good way of learning, particularly a language, as it's always beneficial to hear the language spoken. Look out for the costs involved – you may need to buy several tapes or CDs to complete a course.
- There are computer packages that cover a wide range of subjects. You can also learn computer skills this way.
- Another way to learn is in your own home, through the television and radio. BBC, ITV and Channel 4 transmit educational programmes – for instance, during the BBC's night-time 'Learning Zone'. Sometimes, books and cassettes are available to go with the programmes. There are also on-line resources provided by the BBC. BBC Knowledge is a website and a digital TV channel providing educational material.

Employment-based courses

Increasingly, employers use in-house courses to train their staff – to update skills, learn new skills, to keep abreast of new developments, computer packages etc. The length of these courses varies, but the vast majority are short and tailor made. On the other hand, some very large organisations, such as British Aerospace, have developed their own corporate universities, offering 'virtual' degree courses.

Work-based Learning for Adults (Training for Work in Scotland) is Government-funded training for people aged 25 to 63 who have been unemployed for six months or more.

Individual training plans are drawn up according to need. The plans may include job-specific training or simply basic employability training. Benefits plus an allowance are paid.

CHAPTER 4
The qualification maze

When looking at prospectuses, course directories and databases, the number of different qualifications on offer can be confusing. And, to make matters worse, they are usually known by initials!

- How do these different qualifications relate to each other?
- How can you be sure whether a particular qualification is recognised?
- How can you be certain which is the right qualification for **you**?

Happily, there has been a considerable effort in recent years to introduce more coherence in the qualification system. There is in place a national framework of qualifications for England, Wales and Northern Ireland, and a new framework of qualifications is currently being implemented in Scotland. These frameworks should make it easier to see how any particular qualification you are considering relates to other qualifications, and plot possible progression routes from one qualification level to the next.

Getting to grips with the basics..........

Qualifications range from the **academic**, such as history or English, through to the highly **vocational**. Some vocational courses are fairly broad based e.g. business studies or health and social care, whilst others are specific to a particular occupation e.g. plumbing or accountancy. GCSEs and A levels are examples of academic qualifications; while they do not qualify you for a particular job, they indicate a general level of academic achievement. Qualifications such as NVQs (National Vocational Qualifications), however, relate to a particular occupation.

Qualifications are also divided into a number of different levels, from basic-skill level through to professional-level.

Which qualification?

A checklist of questions

> ➢ Do you want to aim at a general academic qualification, or something work-related?
> ➢ If aiming at work-related qualifications, do you want a broad-based qualification, or a qualification related to a specific occupational area?
> ➢ What level of qualification are you aiming for?
> ➢ Have you the necessary entry requirements (where applicable) or suitable experience to allow you to enter a course at that level?
> ➢ Will any of your previous qualifications or experience give you any exemptions from parts of the course?
> ➢ Is the qualification recognised by employers and relevant professional bodies?
> ➢ Do you need to 'brush up' on any aspects e.g. study skills or maths, prior to starting the course?

This chapter outlines the range of qualifications available across the UK. Qualifications available in England, Wales and Northern Ireland are described initially, followed by a word about accreditation of prior learning, credit transfer schemes and open college networks. The Scottish qualification system is described at the end.

It is, of course, only possible within this book to give a broad outline of the main qualifications available. You can follow up the information provided here by consulting some of the references listed at the end of the chapter, and by talking to course providers and contacting the relevant examining body.

Chapter 4 - The qualification maze

Qualifications in England, Wales and Northern Ireland

To set the scene........

The list below gives you a general idea of the equivalencies between the main available qualifications. As you will see, qualifications are banded into different levels. Please bear in mind that, as academic and vocational qualifications are very different, it is difficult to directly compare them, so only rough indications of equivalence can be made.

Entry level: Certificates of educational achievement

Level 1: GCSEs at grades D-G; Foundation GNVQ; NVQ level 1

Level 2: GCSEs at grades A-C; Intermediate GNVQ; BTEC First Dip/Cert; NVQ level 2

Level 3: GCE A levels; Vocational A levels; BTEC National Dip/Cert; NVQ level 3

Levels 4/5: higher education qualifications, including Higher National Diplomas/Certificates, Diplomas of Higher Education, degrees and postgraduate qualifications; professional qualifications; NVQ levels 4 and 5.

Basic skills and key skills qualifications

Many opportunities are provided for those who need to brush up on their basic literacy and numeracy skills. Courses are often run by adult and community education providers, and through further education colleges. The following are some examples of the available qualifications in basic skills such as literacy and numeracy, and qualifications that relate to the important six key skills of communication, application of number, IT, working with others, problem solving and improving own learning and performance.

> **City and Guilds certificates** – these include the Wordpower and Numberpower Certificates. Each is available at four levels.

- ➢ **OCR Key Skills qualifications** – you can start at a basic level, but then can work your way up, as each of the six key skills can be certified at five levels.
- ➢ **OCR National Skills Profile** – certificates key skills and personal and practical work skills at entry level, related to a number of vocational areas.

A new Key Skills Qualification, available from September 2000, will be awarded to candidates who achieve a pass in the key skills of communication, application of number and information technology, at any level from 1-4. The Qualification is open to all post-16 students, trainees and employees. You have to show what you know, understand and can do in each skill. The certificate awarded will show which level you have achieved for each skill. While being a qualification in its own right, it is expected that the Key Skills Qualification will usually be taken alongside qualifications such as AS and A levels, Vocational A levels and NVQs.

National Vocational Qualifications (NVQs)

National Vocational Qualifications (NVQs) are occupational qualifications, which have been introduced over recent years and now cover almost every area of employment. NVQs are competence-based, meaning that each qualification is assessed on whether you can meet agreed standards in specified skills, tasks or areas of work. Here, compared with academic courses, it may be easier to get credit for previously acquired learning. You gain NVQs not on the basis of time served (as in the old apprenticeship system), nor on the basis of where you were taught, but simply by demonstrating that you are competent in particular skill areas to the required standard. The situation is comparable to learning to drive: the test is not concerned with how long it takes to learn, nor where or how you are taught, but simply on whether you can demonstrate that you can drive to a given standard. It is, therefore, possible to gain an NVQ through assessment in your workplace, without attending a course or sitting any exams.

The NVQ approach has a number of attractive features for adults. It makes it easier to recognise past achievement: you get credit for those skills that you have already acquired both through work and through periods of education and training. It allows you to work towards qualifications over time: each NVQ comprises several units, for which you claim and carry forward credit as you achieve the

Chapter 4 - The qualification maze

required standards. It allows you some choice over how you learn: you can work towards qualifications through a combination of work experience, on-the-job training, private study and attendance at college.

NVQs are awarded at levels 1 to 5 – covering from basic to professional-level skills.

For details of NVQs:

- consult the NVQ database, which may be available in careers centres and adult guidance agencies
- consult the QCA (Qualifications and Curriculum Agency) website: www.qca.org.uk
- contact the relevant National Training Organisation (addresses of relevant NTOs may be listed on careers information, or look at the website www.nto-nc.org)
- your local Training and Enterprise Council (Learning and Skills Council from April 2001) can also provide information.

Kevin Scott – accumulating certificates galore!

'Going back to learning was a must! I left school with no qualifications, which made me unsuccessful in finding employment. I returned to learning to gain some qualifications and to prove to myself that I am more than capable of achieving any given task that is set. To gain qualifications is very important to me, as I want to be able to show a well-deserved CV to anyone whom I might seek employment with. I have been learning for the last seven months. In that time I have achieved higher levels in each subject, which I really never felt possible.

To study to my best capability, I found that I achieve well by being on my own, in the quiet. When I first had to do class talks, I would be really nervous and shake, plus I would talk too fast. But through learning, I have felt more confident and feel that my brain has doubled in size. All the hard work is worth the time and effort. Anyone is capable of achieving what they want, as long as they are committed. Study doesn't mean you have to give up all your spare time; you still have time to have fun!

From going back to learning, I have achieved City and Guilds certifications, as well as OCN and OCR qualifications. Even though I now have some qualifications, I will continue to study, as there is a lot of learning to be learned. Careerwise, I feel that the more I learn and get accredited, the more prosperous my employment will be. Learning has made me see a lot of things in a different light. I just feel like a new person. It's never too late to learn. I promise that you won't be sorry!'

GCSEs

GCSE (General Certificate of Secondary Education) exams are, of course, the academic qualifications taken by young people in their last year of compulsory schooling. They indicate a general level of achievement in a range of academic subjects e.g. English, science, French. As an adult, you can study for a wide range of GCSEs in evening classes run by colleges and adult education centres, or through open and distance learning. A huge range of subjects are on offer, including subjects like psychology, health studies and sociology. You don't need to have studied the subject before. The standard syllabus for students at school lasts two years, but courses available through adult education programmes generally aim for the syllabus to be covered in one year.

Assessment is through a combination of coursework and exams. GCSEs are graded from A* to G; often grades C or above will be sought for entry to higher level courses (although these requirements may be relaxed for adults).

If you are returning to learning, and are looking for a general academic course, GCSEs can be a good starting point.

AS and A levels

GCE A (Advanced) levels are well-known nationally-recognised academic awards which provide entry to a range of jobs and to higher education courses (e.g. university degrees – although, again, the message for adult readers is that A level entry requirements are often relaxed for mature applicants).

In the new structure of A levels (from September 2000), each A level consists of six separate units (in effect, mini-courses). Each unit is separately assessed. The first half of an A level course is made up of three AS (Advanced Subsidiary) units, and successful completion of these leads to an AS level qualification. The second half of the A level course comprises three further units, called A2 units, to complete the A level course.

AS and A levels are available in a similar range of subjects to GCSEs. There are a few subjects (e.g. critical thinking) available at AS level only. Some subjects at AS/A level, such as maths, physics and French, build on the knowledge gained at GCSE (or through equivalent courses). However, there are a number of subjects that you can take at A level which do not require previous knowledge of the subject, such as law, psychology and sociology.

Adults may take AS and A levels through part-time day or evening classes offered by further education colleges and adult education services, or through open or distance learning. AS levels usually take a year to complete, and the full A level takes two years, although some more intensive courses may be available. Assessment is through coursework and exams. While many adults take A levels, adults aiming at entry to higher education may find a specially designed Access course more appropriate.

The Access route

Access courses prepare adults who do not have the necessary qualifications for entry to higher education courses, such as degrees. They provide an alternative to taking A levels, and are specially designed for adults who may not have done any studying for some time, so build in plenty of assistance with developing study skills. Typically, Access courses last one year full-time, and two years part-time. They are usually run through further education colleges, although some are provided by higher education institutions, and adult residential colleges run similar preparatory courses.

Some Access courses prepare students for entry to a broad range of arts and humanities courses, others to science courses. There are also many specific Access courses – geared to entry in a particular subject area, e.g. nursing, social sciences, teaching. Courses often have established links with particular higher education courses.

It is a good idea to check that Access courses of interest to you are 'kitemarked' i.e. approved by the Quality Assurance Agency for Higher Education.

GNVQs (General National Vocational Qualifications) and Vocational A levels

GNVQs are qualifications that tread something of a middle path between occupational qualifications and academic study. They are available at three levels - Foundation, Intermediate and Advanced level (known as Vocational A levels from September 2000). GVNQs and Vocational A levels provide an introduction to 14 broad areas of work. It is possible to progress from one level to the next.

Vocational A levels provide entry to higher education courses or can lead to employment. Under the new structure from September 2000, Vocational A levels are available as a 12-unit qualification - called a Vocational A level (double award) - equivalent to two GCE A levels, and as a 6-unit qualification – a Vocational A level - equivalent to one GCE A level. A 3-unit Vocational A level, called a Vocational AS, is being introduced in four occupational fields.

To date (GNVQs were introduced in the early 1990s) most GNVQ courses have been offered on a full-time basis, both by schools and colleges. Therefore, the majority of students undertaking GNVQ courses have been 16 to 19-year-olds. Whether the new structure will provide more opportunity for these qualifications to be studied on a part-time basis remains to be seen.

BTEC qualifications

BTEC qualifications, awarded by the Edexcel Foundation, are work-related qualifications offered at three levels, First, National and Higher National. They cover a huge range of vocational areas, some are fairly broad e.g. business, building studies; others are very specific e.g. interior design, printing. BTEC qualifications are awarded as Diplomas or Certificates - normally a Diploma is awarded following a full-time course, a Certificate to candidates who study part-time while in employment.

> ➢ **BTEC First** qualifications are at introductory level, normally taken by young people from 16 years.

> ➢ **BTEC National** qualifications are equivalent to two A levels, or level 3 standard, and can provide entry to higher education or employment.

> ➢ **BTEC Higher National** qualifications are at higher education level. They aim to prepare students for work at

Chapter 4 - The qualification maze

technician, supervisory and management level. A year of further study can lead to a degree. The entry qualifications to BTEC Higher National are flexible; usually admissions tutors look for one A level, NVQ level 3, BTEC National, Advanced GNVQ or equivalent, but entry qualifications are generally relaxed for mature applicants with relevant experience.

Other vocational qualifications

There is a range of other work-related qualifications besides those already mentioned. The value of any professional or vocational qualification depends upon its reputation with employers or within a profession. Always be cautious of any diplomas that are awarded by the college itself, rather than by a national body, and check out their acceptability with potential employers.

Some well-regarded vocational qualifications include those awarded by:

- **OCR** (Oxford, Cambridge and RSA Examinations): besides awarding a wide range of academic and vocational qualifications (including NVQs and GNVQs), OCR offers the well-known RSA qualifications of office and business skills.
- **City and Guilds**: provide a wide range of qualifications, related to business and industry (including NVQs and GNVQs). The City and Guilds group includes **Pitman Qualifications** (business and commerce) and **NEBS Management** (supervisory and management qualifications).
- **London Chamber of Commerce and Industry Examinations Board:** LCCI qualifications are offered in all aspects of business, including secretarial and administrative, accounting and management.

Adam Crosby – gaining qualifications whilst working

'I left secondary school with six O levels. I then went on to college to study for my A levels. After about a year the lack of money, and the fact that many of my friends who were working seemed to be enjoying themselves, eventually persuaded me to leave and find work.

I had various jobs - building work, surveying and even antique furniture restoration, none of which offered any long-term security. Finally I decided to join the Civil Service - it offered 'relative' job security, a steady wage and the conditions were reasonable. I looked back upon my year at college and on those people who I still knew who'd completed their courses and gone on to university with a degree of regret for not having done so myself. Many had enjoyed their time in further education. Furthermore, many had gained good jobs through the possibilities their qualifications offered them.

The Civil Service encourages its staff to obtain additional vocational qualifications (giving study leave and part financing of courses). At 23 I decided that I was not too old to 'go back to school'. I'd let myself down to a certain degree by not finishing my education. If opportunities in the job market were to open for me, returning to study was the solution.

My return to learning...

I enrolled on a business and finance ONC (Ordinary National Certificate) course, as it was then called, for two evenings a week; it offered a broad-brush qualification in business (A level equivalent). The first night was a shock (a pleasant one though). The tutors were friendly, the mix of students diverse, both sexes and a good range of ages. The diversity of people meant you never felt like you stood out. You find that some things you know and you can provide help for those that have difficulty, and vice versa.

Another surprising aspect was how easy it was to get to know people - you're all there for the same reason and there was a tendency to conduct group exercises, which forced you to mix with all the students at one time or another. The friendships you strike up are surprising too; some people from that first course (over 10 years ago now) I still know!

In terms of difficulties though, there is the obvious - finding time to fit in a new regime. The course required additional study outside the two evenings. I had to force myself to set aside the time to study. I reduced the amount of time required in the evenings by trying to do most of the work in my lunch hour. The complexity of the course material caused some problems; some students formed small study groups to brainstorm a particular element of the course and if this didn't work, the tutor was always available by telephone and was always glad to help.

Chapter 4 - The qualification maze

Since taking those first tentative steps back into education, I've been hooked. I've done an HNC (Higher National Certificate) in Business & Finance, Chartered Institute of Purchasing & Supply and have just completed the Chartered Institute of Management Accountants qualification.

The Civil Service is a large organisation offering a lot of job diversity. I'm still in it having had jobs in buying, contracts, computer programming and now in accountancy. The qualifications have opened up career opportunities I'd never have had, and enabled me to try different jobs and earn more money (something most of us are interested in).

Besides the career benefits, returning to education has provided me with a greater insight into my own abilities, more confidence and friends I might never otherwise have known.

Some words of advice to prospective learners......

Returning to learning is a big step for anyone, especially if you've been out of education long time. Don't rush into it. If you've got a family, or are in a relationship, make sure they understand and support you - it will mean sacrificing some of the time you spend with them.

Make sure you can afford the time to do it. You'll likely feel at some point you haven't got the time and it's getting too much. If this happens, speak to those close to you, speak to your course tutor (they can often help with rescheduling work) and speak to others in your class; they can often help you get round a problem.

Form a study group (it need only be two or three of you) - try to get together every week or two. You'll find it enables you to get another person's perspective on an issue or problem. It's also an excuse to get out!!! Meet at each other's house or a quiet pub.

Plan - most courses have a timetable you must work to. It will probably contain homework or project deadlines - use this to structure your study time. Try to set aside a set amount of time each day or two and try to stick to it. Once you get in the routine it becomes easier (honest).

Finally, never put off a problem; share it. It is unlikely that your problem is unique - tell someone about it! Even if they can't help, they can certainly understand and offer encouragement.'

Diplomas of Higher Education (DipHE)

These are higher education qualifications requiring two years' full-time study. Students who successfully complete a DipHE may take a further year of study to top up to a degree. There are many fewer DipHE courses than degree courses. It is possible to take a DipHE in academic subjects, such as history and English; often courses leading to DipHE are covering more than one subject e.g DipHE in geography and tourism, psychology and health, in combined studies, for example. Some professional courses in vocational areas like nursing and youth work also lead to a DipHE award. Entry requirements are as for a degree.

Certificates in Higher Education may be awarded after the equivalent of one year of study at higher education level.

Degrees

A degree is the standard entry requirement for many professional and managerial careers. The award of a degree has wide currency and opens many doors. The range of subjects available is immense, ranging from the highly academic, such as classical studies, through to the highly vocational, such as town and country planning. Some are very broad-based, e.g. combined studies, while others are very specialised e.g. animation. Degrees require at least three years' study, longer if you study on a part-time basis. Some are offered as sandwich courses, with study interspersed with spells in industry and commerce. Many degrees are structured on a modular basis, allowing you to choose what topics to study, specialising as you go along.

Higher education establishments welcome mature students (usually defined as entrants aged 21 or over) and entry requirements may be relaxed.(The stated minimum requirements for entry by young people are two A levels or equivalent, plus supporting GCSEs.) As a mature applicant, admissions tutors will want to satisfy themselves that you have the ability to cope with the demands of the course. They will therefore look at what you have achieved in the past, and some evidence of recent study is also important. Many adult students prepare themselves by following a specially designed Access course (as described on page 51).

Foundation degrees

The Government has recently proposed the introduction of foundation degrees. These will be in vocational subjects, designed particularly to meet the skill requirements of industry and commerce. Foundation degrees will be delivered flexibly, to meet the needs of people who wish to combine study with employment. They will therefore be available through full- and part-time study and through distance learning. Studying full-time, the degree will take two years to complete. While it is intended that a foundation degree will be a well-regarded qualification in its own right, it will be possible to achieve an honours degree through one year's further study and participation in a summer school. The first foundation degrees are scheduled to start in Autumn 2001.

Postgraduate awards

Postgraduate courses divide into three broad categories: Master's degrees and doctorates, which are both higher degrees, and postgraduate diplomas or certificates.

The number of **Master's degree courses** has mushroomed in recent years. For example, MBA (Master of Business Administration) programmes are now commonplace. Many master's degrees are 'taught masters', requiring, typically, a year's full-time study including a dissertation or extended work-based project. Many are designed for people with some work and professional experience rather than new graduates. Other Master's degrees are awarded following a research project.

Postgraduate diplomas and certificates are usually vocational awards. Some may be required for entry to particular professions, e.g. the PGCE for entry to teaching.

Doctorate degrees (e.g. PhDs) are awarded after doing several years' research in a particular subject.

Professional bodies

Many professional bodies set their own examinations and qualifications. Achieving their qualifications leads to membership of that particular professional body, and is often obligatory if you want to enter a particular career, or to progress to a further level within a particular field of work. For example, to work in town planning, you need to complete a course accredited by the Royal Town Planning Institute. Professional qualifications are gradually being brought into the NVQ structure, although most remain outside it. This does not make them any less valuable, it simply reflects that they are not organised in a way that meets NVQ criteria.

Jean Ingham – still learning and gaining qualifications in semi-retirement

'I am currently semi-retired - in body but not in mind - and find I need an interest to focus on.

Over the years, I have retained my interest in further education - twenty years ago (after being widowed) I took a full-time Training Opportunities (TOPS) course for a year. I thoroughly enjoyed returning to study and obtaining qualifications in shorthand and typing, and taking RSAs in English, commerce, business studies etc. This enabled me to obtain a post as a school secretary, which was ideal when my daughters were growing up.

Ten years ago I took an A level in English Literature and this was another highlight; trips to see productions of 'Taming of the Shrew' at Stratford-upon-Avon and the Barbican opened up another world. Studying 20th Century English Poetry meant I discovered Philip Larkin! 'What are days for…?'

I have recently completed an Adult Basic Education Certificate in Literacy, an area in which I've always had an interest. I have been surprised at how intensive the course has been, but appreciate that 'volunteer helpers' must be aware of the difficulties many people still face in everyday situations, if they are unable to read or write adequately. I have already been helping at a weekly class - a mixed group of people with varying needs and have been impressed by the relaxed and almost social atmosphere which prevails. One of my most enjoyable experiences has been observing a class of people with learning disabilities, who were interested and keen to learn.

I know I shall gain a lot from my 'weekly two-hourly volunteering slot' and hopefully the students will too!'

Accreditation of prior learning

You may get credit towards (or exemption from) part of courses, for previous study or less formal learning that you have undertaken. Unlike the waiving of standard entry requirements, this necessarily requires a more involved process. In colleges and universities, this process is known by one of two acronyms, APL - the Accreditation of Prior Learning or APEL - the Accreditation of Prior Experiential Learning. APL and APEL can therefore give you recognition or 'credit' for the skills and knowledge that you have already gained.

Typically, you will be required to complete a portfolio with supporting documentation to demonstrate that you have acquired the relevant knowledge and learning. You might also be required to undergo a number of assessments. It may not always be worth going through this process, as it can be lengthy and it may be expensive.

However, it is always worth asking whether any relevant previous study and experience you may have can be formerly recognised. It could save repeating areas of study you have already covered.

Credit Accumulation and Transfer Schemes

CATS schemes, as they are known, operate in many universities and higher education colleges. Courses are increasingly 'modularised' i.e. broken down into separate modules or mini-courses, as described in chapter three. Each module is worth a number of credit points, usually rated at a particular level. You build up your total of credit points by completing individual modules, until you gain sufficient credit points at the correct levels to be awarded a particular qualification.

This system allows you the flexibility to change courses, for example, without necessarily losing 'credit' for what you have achieved so far. It can also allow you to swap between full- and part-time study. If you wish, or need to, move to another institution or take a break from study, the CATS system allows you to retain and transfer credit for the modules that you have already passed. CATS also offers more opportunities within a course; your degree course may require you to take certain core subjects but you may be able to take a much wider range of optional modules providing you accumulate sufficient credit points for the degree. Previous study that you have undertaken may also be assessed and given credit points.

At higher education level, Scotland has one scheme (SCOTCAT), while there are a variety of schemes operating in the rest of the UK. Enquire about such schemes at any colleges or universities to which you are thinking of applying.

Open College Networks (OCNs)

Open College Networks accredit qualifications offered through colleges and other learning providers in their particular geographical area. There are over thirty local Networks in operation across England, Wales and Northern Ireland.

OCNs accredit courses from basic level through to Access courses. They offer you a way to get credit for learning that you may have done on a formal course, in the workplace, through a training programme or via voluntary work. The National Open College Network operates a framework of four levels of achievement. Each credit awarded represents 30 hours of learning, and is accredited at one of four levels. You can build up credits as you study, at a level appropriate to you. Such accreditation systems allow accreditation of learning that may not be formerly certificated elsewhere, and make it easier to progress from one learning opportunity to another. It makes for much easier comparison between courses.

Peter Walters – proving its never too late to gain more qualifications!

'I joined a full-time course that consisted of three sessions of English a week, two of maths and computers and some part-time cooking, carpentry and soft-toy making. At secondary school I was educated to CSE level in English and history, and that was it really. Trouble was, I knew it all, so why bother learning?

How times change. This time round (in my late thirties) I was not only eager to learn, I was hungry for it too. Janet, my English tutor, put me forward for an OCR exam. I was apprehensive, but passed with a credit. I also passed my first maths OCR exam - not bad for someone who was in the bottom set in school all those years earlier.

However, the real 'buzz' for me came in computing. A complete novice, I was pessimistic about my chances of coming to terms with a PC. However, the more you learn the more confident you become. To date, I have two computing exams, two English exams and am eagerly awaiting the result of my second OCR exam in maths. I am hopeful I will get a credit in this!'

Chapter 4 - The qualification maze

Scottish qualifications

Scottish qualifications are currently undergoing far-reaching changes; these are due to be completed by 2002. Basically, a new framework of National Qualifications is being implemented, organised into five levels:

- Access
- Intermediate 1
- Intermediate 2
- Higher
- Advanced Higher.

The idea is that subjects are available at each of the five levels, and students can move up to the next level of difficulty on successful completion of their current level. The system can allow for people to study at different levels in different subjects.

Standard Grades

This is the equivalent qualification to GCSE, offered in a similar range of subjects. Adults may take Standard Grades through further education colleges. Assessment is normally through a mixture of formal examination and assessed coursework. Standard Grades are not affected by the current reforms, but for a rough comparison, Standard Grade General Level (grades 3 and 4) requires roughly the same level of competence as Intermediate 1, and Standard Grade Credit Level (grades 1 and 2) as Intermediate 2.

National Qualifications at Higher level

Scottish Higher Grades have traditionally been taken after one year of further study following Standard Grades, and provide entry to Scottish universities. Highers are available in a wide range of academic subjects. The current Highers are being replaced from 2000 by new national qualifications at Higher level, which have equivalent value to the old Highers.

National Qualifications at Advanced Higher level

This is a new qualification, replacing the Certificate of Sixth Year Studies by 2002. While following on from Highers, the Advanced

Higher is a free-standing qualification, so you do not need to have completed the Higher course before starting the Advanced Higher.

National Units, Courses and Group Awards

> **National Units** are available over a wide range of vocational fields. Most Units are 40-hours long, although some are 20, and others possibly 80. They are assessed by teachers and lecturers on a pass or fail basis.

> **National Courses** are made up of, usually, three 40-hour national units, plus time for preparing for an external assessment.

> **Scottish Group Awards (SGAs)** are made up of groupings of National Units and National Courses. They can be taken over one year full-time, or part-time over a longer period. There are Scottish Group Awards available at each of the five levels listed above.

NB. GSVQs (General Scottish Vocational Qualifications) are being phased out.

Scottish Vocational Qualifications (SVQs)

These are the counterpart to NVQs offered elsewhere in the UK, and operate on a similar basis. SVQs are available over a wide range of occupational fields.

Scottish Qualifications Certificate (SQC)

A new certificate, the **Scottish Qualifications Certificate**, is being introduced to replace the Scottish Certificate of Education (SCE) and Record of Education and Training (RET). The new Certificate will comprise a complete record of a student's achievements, listing all types of qualifications gained.

Further information

QCA (Qualifications and Curriculum Authority) - 29 Bolton Street, London W1Y 7PD. Tel: 020 7509 5555. Covers England, Wales and Northern Ireland. Information about academic and vocational qualifications can be found on their website: www.qca.org.uk

Chapter 4 - The qualification maze

SQA (Scottish Qualifications Authority) – based at Ironmills Road, Dalkeith, Midlothian EH22 1LE and at Hanover House, 24 Douglas Street, Glasgow G2 7NQ. The SQA helpline is: 0141 242 2214. Their website also contains information about qualifications: www.sqa.org.uk

Basic Skills Agency – Commonwealth House, 1-19 New Oxford Street, London WC1A 1NU. Tel: 020 7405 4017.

The Agency operates a free helpline: 0800 700 987. This is for anyone who wants to be put in touch with a local basic skills course. It covers England and Wales. Website: www.basic-skills.co.uk

National Open College Network – University of Derby, Kedleston Road, Derby DE22 1GB. Tel: 01332 622712. Website: www.nocn.ac.uk

The following resources may be available in careers centres, adult guidance agencies and public reference libraries. The list contains comprehensive reference books which are more likely to be found in libraries, and handbooks.

British Qualifications – a reference directory of educational, technical, professional and academic qualifications. Lists qualifications by trades and professions and contains details of professional institutions and accrediting bodies. Published by Kogan Page

British Vocational Qualifications – comprehensive reference to vocational qualifications. Published by Kogan Page.

International Guide to Qualifications in Education – published by Cassell.

DOFE Directory of Further Education – published annually by Hobsons. Covers further education courses across the UK.

NVQs and How to Get Them – published by Kogan Page, £8.99.

How to Choose Your GCSEs – published by Trotman, £8.99.

Which A levels? – published by Lifetime Careers Publishing, £10.99.

University and College Entrance: the Official Guide – published annually by UCAS; lists courses across the UK leading to degrees, HNDs and DipHEs.

Coming Back to Learning

CHAPTER 5
Finding the right provider

All providers of learning opportunities produce a range of publications to advertise and describe their courses. It is usually easy enough to obtain a fair selection, at the cost of a few telephone calls, but making some sense of it all is less easy. Even if you know what type of course you want to do, tracking down a training provider, college, university or education centre that provides exactly what you want, making an application and getting accepted can be a time-consuming process.

This chapter provides you with a guide to the different types of institutions, from adult education services through to universities; it covers what they provide, who to contact for advice and further information and how to apply for courses. It is preceded by more general advice on getting information. The chapter concludes with a word about study and training abroad.

Working through the information maze

Prime sources of information about learning opportunities are the providers themselves. They produce a great deal of material advertising their courses and services. But ringing round local colleges can take time. Of course, you can also find an increasing amount of information on providers' websites, if you have access to the Internet, but again, you need to know where to start looking. It is obviously preferable to target those institutions that run the sort of courses that you wish to take.

One short cut is to take advantage of the fact that some organisations have done part of the work for you.

> **Adult information, advice and guidance agencies, careers service libraries** and other advisory agencies (featured in Chapter two) will hold stocks of leaflets, prospectuses and brochures. They also may offer access to local and national course databases and local, regional and national directories of learning opportunities.

> Most **public libraries** will have an education section and a notice board advertising courses and coming events. They are also likely to have many of the national directories of education and training.

> **learndirect** is the national telephone helpline for any adult wanting information about learning opportunities of any type; their freephone number is **0800 100 900**. Lines are open from 9.00 am to 9.00 pm Monday to Friday, and until 12 noon on Saturdays.

> It is also worth keeping a lookout for any local 'education fairs', 'education and training roadshows' and similar events that may be put on in your locality. These provide an opportunity to talk directly to providers of courses. Local newspapers also sometimes do special features on learning opportunities - especially around the main enrolment season for educational institutions – late August/early September.

With assistance from such sources, you can identify possible courses of interest, and start to make a shortlist of those most likely to be of direct interest. You may live within easy travelling distance of several education and training providers. If you include all local colleges, adult education centres and private education and training organisations, then you may have a wide choice of providers. Do not be discouraged if the first provider you approach cannot deliver the goods. By considering all the options, you greatly increase your chances of finding a suitable course near to you. Even in rural areas, you might be surprised at the number of providers within reachable distance.

An overview of providers

> The major providers of learning opportunities are the **public sector colleges and universities**. They offer a huge

Chapter 5 - Finding the right provider

range of courses at every level. They receive public funding towards their costs; fees are payable by adult students but some students may get fee remission, or assistance towards their fees – see Chapter six.

➢ There are also **independent providers** of education and training, operating on a commercial basis, although some are registered educational charities. The opportunities provided through the independent, or private, sector also cover a wide range of subject areas, from basic to professional level.

➢ The Government provides **work-based learning** opportunities for unemployed people. The training is delivered through various agencies, under contract. Many independent learning providers are contracted to provide government-funded training.

➢ Learning opportunities can also be provided by **voluntary organisations**, and other community based, non-profit making bodies.

➢ **Employers**, of course, provide learning opportunities for their staff; for many employees, this includes the opportunity to gain qualifications.

➢ Many **professional bodies** offer work-related qualifications for their field of work.

When researching information about learning opportunities, it helps if you are aware of the distinction between further education and higher education:

➢ **Further education** is learning at non-advanced level i.e. up to level 3 (A level standard). This includes NVQ and GNVQ courses, and other vocational and academic courses. Further education courses can be taken on a full- or part-time basis, including through open and distance learning. Further education courses differ enormously in the time they take, from a few weeks to, say, two years.

➢ **Higher education** is learning at a standard beyond level 3. It embraces diplomas, degrees, professional qualifications and postgraduate awards. Studying for these awards requires a sustained commitment. Most undergraduate degree courses, for example, require three years' full-time study. That does not mean you have to be a full-time student, there are increasing opportunities to study on a part-time basis, but all options will require a substantial investment in time.

What can cause confusion is that many further education colleges provide opportunities both at further **and** at higher education level.

The providers

The following providers of education and training are described:

- adult and community education
- voluntary organisations
- Workers' Educational Association (WEA)
- U3A
- learning at work – employers and trade union-based learning
- UfI learndirect centres
- Government-funded learning programmes for unemployed adults
- colleges of further education
- adult residential colleges
- universities and colleges of higher education
- the Open University
- independent providers - including independent open/ distance learning providers.

Adult and community education

Each year more than a million students take evening or short daytime courses through adult and community education. A wide variety of general interest courses for recreation and personal development are available. These may include 'return to study' courses and basic skills courses (literacy and numeracy), GCSE courses and AS and A levels. Basic vocational qualifications, such as RSA, may also be on offer.

Adult and community education can be offered through:

Chapter 5 - Finding the right provider

> adult and community education centres, run by local education authorities
> colleges of further education
> community colleges or community schools
> the extra-mural departments of universities.

The philosophy of adult and community education services is to make courses open and accessible to all. Many services make considerable efforts to provide advice and guidance prior to enrolment, to run crèches and to accommodate the needs of people with disabilities. Booking is made simple, either by telephone, post or by direct application at various centres during enrolment days (or weeks). A policy of 'first come, first served' usually applies.

Fees vary, but have risen over recent years as local authority expenditure is increasingly squeezed. Generally, adult education courses need to cover their costs, and the fees are based on a viable number of enrolments. You might expect to pay £2-£3 an hour for leisure/non vocational courses. Courses leading to certification are generally more expensive. Many courses have concessionary rates to those on benefits or low incomes. Basic education courses are normally free.

Overall responsibility for the funding of adult and community education in England will be taken over, from April 2001, by local Learning and Skills Councils. These Councils will, in partnership with local education authorities, develop future arrangements for adult and community education.

Adult and community education operates from a variety of premises, often in local schools, and under a number of identities. To get details for your area, contact your local education authority and ask for the department which deals with adult and community education. Your local library and adult information and guidance agencies should also be able to advise, of course.

Voluntary organisations

Many charities, voluntary bodies and community organisations run education and training courses. For some, such as Shelter, which runs courses for voluntary and statutory workers in housing and care work, it is a natural extension of their other activities. For others, like the Workers' Educational Association, which is perhaps the best-known voluntary provider, education is the primary activity.

Voluntary organisations tend to specialise in particular disciplines or cater for a specific clientele, rather than duplicating the type of courses readily available from colleges, universities or commercial training companies. Many voluntary bodies are local rather than national, meeting the needs of particular communities.

Many voluntary bodies provide well-respected training, and for some, such as Relate or the Samaritans, thorough and in-depth training of volunteers is of crucial importance. Increasingly, the training offered through voluntary organisations is becoming formally accredited, often through local Open College Networks (see page 66).

While there is no national directory of voluntary organisations involved in education and training, you will find that most organisations offer some kind of training. However, many bodies have a precarious future as the sector is heavily dependent on sponsorship, short-term grants and (increasingly limited) local and central government funding. The places to look for information about organisations active in your area are your local volunteer bureaux, public libraries, community centres and guidance centres.

The National Centre for Volunteering – The Information Service, Regent's Wharf, 8 All Saints Street, London N1 9RL. Tel: 020 7520 8900. Covers England. Publishes a variety of information sheets, including one called *Accreditation of Voluntary Work*; also publish *The Spirit of Volunteering* – a guide to getting into volunteering (send an A4 stamped (33p) addressed envelope). Website: www.volunteering.org.uk

Workers' Educational Association (WEA)

Founded in 1903, the WEA, an independent organisation and a registered charity, provides part-time education for adults. It runs courses both for groups of individuals and for collective bodies such as trade unions, community organisations and women's groups. The association aims to bring education to the widest community, with 'a particular concern for the socially, economically or educationally disadvantaged'.

The WEA is organised on a regional basis, with about 700 local branches throughout the UK. It is a democratic body, open to all; members have a say in what courses each branch runs, and students are consulted on course content and teaching methods. Individual course programmes therefore vary from area to area, but typically the WEA courses cover:

Chapter 5 - Finding the right provider

- academic and liberal studies - such as philosophy, economics, literature
- trade union education
- women's education
- creative arts
- second-chance-to-learn or return-to-study programmes
- community education - working with housing associations, unemployed groups and other voluntary organisations.

Courses are open to all; once you enrol on a course you automatically become a member. Fees usually have to cover the costs of running the course. Courses aimed particularly at those who are unemployed or disadvantaged are usually free.

Detailed information about local WEA activities can be obtained from local branches or district offices; get contact addresses from libraries or the phone directory, or via their website.

WEA National Office: Temple House, 17 Victoria Park Square, London E2 9PB. Tel: 020 8983 1515. Website: www.wea.org.uk

U3A

The U3A – University of the Third Age – was started in the UK in 1982. It is an organisation created to encourage lifelong learning, for those who are no longer in full-time employment. There are more than 400 groups. U3A members organise learning groups themselves, using the skills of the members to organise and teach. The subjects tackled vary according to the interests and skills of the group, and range from local history or foreign languages to computing.

You don't need any qualifications to join a group, and each member pays a small annual membership fee. Your local library should be able to provide contact details of your local group, or consult the U3A website.

U3A National Office: 26 Harrison Street, London WC1H 8JG. Tel: 020 837 8833. Website: www.u3a.org.uk

Learning at work

Much of the learning undertaken by adults relates to their employment, and is supported by their employers. Trade unions also play an important role in developing opportunities for workplace learning. Learning opportunities available range from basic skills through to those at professional level. The Government have placed great emphasis on encouraging employers to provide quality training to their workforce – in order to equip employees with the skills and qualifications needed for a successful future economy.

Employers

Many, particularly larger employers, have well-established staff training and development programmes.

> These may involve employees working towards nationally-recognised qualifications, such as NVQs, which can be gained through assessment in the workplace.

> Employees may follow the traditional pattern of attending part-time courses at local further education colleges - perhaps a half day and evening a week, for example.

> Some staff gain qualifications through distance learning. Such courses may be provided through colleges, universities, independent providers or professional bodies.

> A few employers have learndirect centres (see below) based in their premises, for the benefit of employees.

If you are employed, your employer could support your training through paying course fees, contributing to your individual learning account (ILA) – see page 118 – and/or allowing you paid or unpaid time off to attend a course or open learning centre. If you are in work and wish to gain further work-related qualifications, find out what support may be available.

If you are planning a return to work, when looking for jobs check what training opportunities may be open to you, especially if you wish to build on learning you have done prior to re-entering the workplace. There are a few large employers which run employee assistance programmes not only for work-related courses, but for any learning opportunity of the employee's choice.

Trade union-based learning

Trade unions have long been involved in encouraging employees to develop their skills and qualifications, and in providing learning opportunities. In 1998, TUC Learning Services was established to help unions and their members to increase participation in workplace learning.

An important element of this has been the setting up of a Union Learning Fund. Over 40 projects were initially funded, which covered a variety of different approaches to increasing employees' participation in learning. These have included the setting up of workplace learning centres, so providing staff easy access to flexible open learning courses, and developing new ways of delivering courses, such as through the Internet with online tutor support.

In addition, a trained network of union learning representatives is being developed, to provide advice and guidance to employees.

There are, therefore, tremendous opportunities for furthering your skills and qualifications through employment, supported by your employer. Don't feel you have to do it all before you enter work!

learndirect centres

learndirect centres are a new initiative, currently being set up through the University for Industry (UfI). Learndirect centres offer access to learning which is delivered via computers and the Internet – i.e. you use a computer to work through a learning package, at times and at a pace that suits you. It is therefore a very flexible way of learning.

The plan is to establish a national network of learndirect centres. The first learndirect centres opened in Autumn 1999. There are currently 251 centres across England, Wales and Northern Ireland. The network will be fully in place and operational by Autumn 2000. In Scotland, a similar initiative is taking place, where a network of centres will be launched from October 2000.

learndirect centres are run by a variety of organisations that have contracted to operate them. This includes colleges, employers, trade unions, voluntary organisations and so on. It is intended that learndirect centres should be found in a variety of settings, such as community centres, libraries and shopping centres, which are easily accessible to the public. For example, a learndirect centre was recently opened at St Helens Rugby League Club, running IT and business skills courses. It is run by St Helens College together with the Rugby League, and is open to anyone across the community who wants to learn new skills. Some centres are based in companies, for the benefit of their employees. It is also possible to undertake learndirect courses at home, if you have your own computer.

There are about 300 courses currently on offer. Some courses are web-based, so you need an Internet link to access them. Others are accessed via a CD-Rom. Paper-based materials and workbooks will also be used for some courses. Courses include IT courses e.g. on wordprocessing, databases, computerised accounts systems, etc. There are also courses covering basic skills, customer service, business skills and management. Courses range from basic to postgraduate level. The number and range of approved courses are increasing all the time.

Some students are able to get help towards fees, you should enquire at your nearest learndirect centre.

To find out about your nearest learndirect centre, and about available courses, telephone the learndirect helpline: 0800 100 900.

Further information can also be found on the following websites:

www.learndirect.co.uk

www.ufitld.co.uk (for information about England, Wales and N.I.)

www.scottishufi.co.uk (for information about Scotland)

Government-funded learning programmes for unemployed adults

There are a number of Government-funded training opportunities for unemployed adults, operating across the UK. The programmes aim to equip adults with work-related skills and qualifications. Eligibility to join such programmes depends on how long you have been unemployed, or on your personal circumstances. The rules are quite complex, so the starting point for further information on eligibility and what is available in your locality is your local Jobcentre.

The main programmes currently running are described below. Please bear in mind that such programmes are always subject to change, especially over the next year or two, as new bodies take over responsibility for some programmes.

The New Deal

The New Deal is the Government's main programme to help people get back into employment. There are separate programmes for those aged 18-24, for people aged 25+, for those aged 50+, for lone parents, for those with disabilities and for partners of unemployed people.

Chapter 5 - Finding the right provider

A variety of options are available under each New Deal programme; many are concerned with helping people to find employment, but included under some programmes are opportunities for full-time education and training.

Under the **New Deal for those aged 25+**, full-time work-related education and training for up to a year is a possible option for those whose lack of skills and qualifications are making it difficult for them to find work. Eligibility for this programme is normally for those who have been claiming Jobseekers' Allowance (JSA) for two years or more, or 18 months or more in Northern Ireland and in particular areas of England, Scotland and Wales, where some pilot projects are in operation. If you have a disability, you also may qualify to join this programme. (Check with the Jobcentre for details of eligibility.) While undertaking full-time education and training, you would still receive JSA. The education and training option is mainly aimed at people who have not yet gained NVQ qualifications up to level 3.

The **New Deal for those aged 18-24** is open to those who have been claiming Jobseekers' Allowance for six months or more. Full-time education and training is also an option under this programme.

The programme for **partners** of unemployed people receiving Jobseekers' Allowance includes the chance to take short refresher courses or to train for something new.

Work-based Learning for Adults (WbLA)

This programme is offered in England, currently operating under the auspices of Training and Enterprise Councils (TECs) and Chambers of Commerce, Training and Enterprise (CCTEs). From April 2001, responsibility for the programme will be taken over by the Employment Service (and it is possible that the programme will be incorporated within New Deal). A similar programme is currently available in Wales. In Scotland, **Training for Work** is the equivalent programme, which runs along broadly similar lines, and is the responsibility of Local Enterprise Companies (LECs).

Currently, Work-based Learning for Adults is open to people aged 25 to 63, who have been registered unemployed for six months or more. However, various other people who have not been registered as unemployed for this period are also eligible. This includes people with disabilities, returners to the labour market (who have been out of work for more than two years for domestic reasons), lone parents, those who have lost their job through large-scale redundancy, Armed Forces leavers, ex-offenders and those who need basic skills training in literacy and numeracy or help with spoken English.

In 1999, approximately 15% of people starting on Work-based Learning for Adults were aged 50 or more.

Each person joining the programme follows an individual training plan, according to their needs. This could include work experience with an employer, the chance to gain NVQs, job specific training and basic employability training. Help with basic skills (literacy and numeracy) may be included. While most people follow the programme full-time, it can be possible to train part-time. Special aids or adapted equipment may be provided for people who have special needs.

While on the programme, you get an allowance equivalent to any benefits you are currently receiving, plus £10 a week. There may also be extra help for travelling expenses.

Advanced Modern Apprenticeships

Advanced Modern Apprenticeships provide work-based training leading to NVQ level 3 across a wide range of career areas. They are aimed at young people. Trainees are normally employed. Training, which usually takes three years, must be completed by the age of 25. It is therefore possible for a 21-year-old to start such an apprenticeship, although in practice, most apprentices are younger on entry.

Contact your local Jobcentre, TEC, CCTE or LEC for information about the range of training opportunities for unemployed people.

Jobcentre Services – an Employment Service booklet which includes information about the above programmes.

The Government's New Deal website provides information about the full range of options under New Deal: www.newdeal.gov.uk

---

Richard Griffiths – found a job through work-based training

> '*After leaving college, although I was well qualified, I had difficulty finding work due to my lack of work experience. After being unemployed for two years, in January 1999 I was referred to Spring Skills through the Employment Service, as part of the Government's*

Chapter 5 - Finding the right provider

Work-Based Training for Adults scheme. I joined as a trainee; working in the company's IT training room.

I was shortly moved to work in the reception area, to gain work experience in administration. Here I was taught general office skills, and how to use the computer system. After two months of intense general office skills, I became employed with Spring Skills as a full-time administrator.

I feel that working at Spring Skills, holding down a responsible position, has boosted my self-confidence tremendously. Receiving a proper salary after being on benefit for some time is another obvious bonus. Whilst working for Spring Skills, I was also offered the chance to gain an NVQ level 3 in business administration, which is sure to help me in the future.

Spring Skills gave me great support whilst re-training, and, as a result of my job here, I now have a much wider range of practical skills and experience with which to further my career.'

Colleges of further education

The further education sector is a major provider of education for adults. As mentioned earlier in this chapter, further education comprises education up to level 3, i.e. courses up to A level standard/ NVQ level 3. In 1999, 72% of students in England enrolling on further education courses leading to a qualification were aged 19 or older; 11% of these were on full-time courses. Adults are therefore becoming ever more important to colleges.

There are more than 500 further education colleges across the UK. Most colleges run courses across a wide range of subjects leading to academic and vocational qualifications, from basic education and refresher courses in subjects like English and maths, through to courses at higher education level. Some colleges specialise in particular disciplines such as agriculture, art, building or food technology. Many colleges also provide a full programme of leisure and recreational courses for adults. Although now independent of local authority control and financed by national funding bodies, further education colleges retain strong ties with their local communities.

College names can be confusing because there is no consistency or standard convention. Whether your local college is called Townsville College of Further Education, Townsville Regional College, Townsville College of Arts and Technology, or just plain Townsville College, it is likely to offer much the same broad range of courses. Specialist colleges, such as Townsville College of Art, tend to be self-evident.

Flexibility and ease of access

One of the reasons colleges are successful at attracting large numbers of mature students is because they make a virtue out of being flexible. There has always been a strong tradition of part-time courses in the further education sector. Many courses are run during evenings or on a day-release basis. Modular programmes enable students to work towards qualifications step by step.

In recent years, colleges have made great efforts to reach more people. A range of courses to encourage adults back into education have been offered, such as 'return to learn' and similarly titled courses. Many colleges have set up open or flexible learning centres; these are particularly useful if you are unable to attend college on a regular basis, allowing you to study independently at home or in college on a drop-in basis using open learning packages (see chapter three). Other colleges have 'moved into the community', running courses in outstations and community centres. Some have developed courses that are particularly appropriate for those with special needs – with, for example, specialist computing facilities designed for those with particular needs. Most colleges offer crèches and day nurseries. And you don't necessarily have to enrol in September as more courses are now run all year round.

Certain courses offered by some colleges are made available to learners on a distance-learning basis.

Wide range of qualifications

At further education colleges you can study for a wide range of qualifications and awards, both academic and vocational. These include a wide range of qualifications offered by professional bodies, such as the Chartered Institute of Marketing, Association of Accounting Technicians, or the International Therapy Examination Council.

Chapter 5 - Finding the right provider

Routes to higher education

Most advanced qualifications (beyond level 3 or A level standard) are delivered within the realm of higher education institutions. However, further education colleges have always provided a limited range of higher education courses, mostly at Higher National Diploma level e.g. HND Business Studies, Travel and Tourism Management and Engineering. Most further education colleges have significantly expanded the range of higher education courses they offer in recent years, including at degree level. FE colleges are also the major providers of Access courses, which prepare adults without formal qualifications for entry to universities and higher education colleges (see chapter four).

Colleges of further education are able to offer degree courses through franchising arrangements with universities. Sometimes the college is able to offer the first year of the degree, sometimes the whole of the degree course. This enables students to take either the first stages of a university course, or the whole of it, at a local college. These arrangements usually reflect geographical ties; for example, Sheffield Hallam University has links with colleges in Wakefield, Barnsley, Rotherham, Huddersfield and Chesterfield as well as in Sheffield itself. 1000 students are on Sheffield Hallam's 'outreach' learning programmes, delivered through these colleges. The outreach programmes available include one-year foundation courses (i.e. a preparatory year prior to moving on to the first year of a particular degree course), and parts of diploma and degree courses.

This linking of further and higher education institutions can be of huge benefit to adult learners with home and family commitments whose local town does not have a university. Such arrangements can make the difference between higher education being a viable option or not.

Entry requirements to higher education courses are generally flexible for adults. Colleges are prepared to take into account previous experience whether it is in (paid or voluntary) work, at home or in education (see accreditation of prior learning, page 64). The test is whether the applicant will benefit from the course, and guidance staff will sometimes recommend preparatory or foundation programmes where appropriate.

To find out what your local college can offer, contact their **admissions and guidance units**. Most colleges produce separate part- and full-time prospectuses; some produce separate prospectuses listing courses at higher education level. Most also have websites listing their courses. Some colleges have mature students' advisers (or guidance counsellors) who can advise both on courses and the practicalities of returning to study.

DOFE - Directory of Further Education - a region by region guide to further education, with details of over 75,000 courses across the UK. Published annually by Hobsons, and available in most libraries and careers centres.

Adult residential colleges

Adult residential colleges offer an alternative way of returning to academic education and preparing for study at a higher level. They provide a relaxed environment in which to live, work and learn, and they may be particularly, suitable for people who left school early or with few qualifications. There are eight colleges across the UK, each with a distinctive academic programme, although mainly in social sciences and the humanities. In addition to their residential programmes, some of the colleges also run part-time and short courses. The colleges welcome and cater for adults of all ages. The minimum age of entry varies between 20 and 21. There are no formal entry qualifications for most courses; instead, selection is by interview and sometimes some written work. Adult education bursaries are available for full-time residential courses which cover course fees, provide funding towards living expenses and some assistance with travel expenses. Each college has details about which courses and which students are eligible for this support. More information about the bursary system is provided in chapter six.

Further information can be obtained directly from each college.

Coleg Harlech runs a Diploma in General Studies on a full- or part-time basis, providing university-level entrance. Also offers short courses. Contact: Coleg Harlech, Harlech, Gwynedd LL46 2PU. Tel: 01766 780363. Website: www.harlech.ac.uk

Co-operative College offers a 21-week residential Certificate in Policy Studies, which is recognised for access to higher education. Contact: Co-operative College, Stanford Hall, Loughborough LE12 5QR. Tel: 01509 857204. Website: www.coop-college.ac.uk

Fircroft College runs a one-year access programme, and various short courses. Contact: Fircroft College of Adult Education, 1018 Bristol Road, Selly Oak, Birmingham B29 6LH Tel: 0121 472 0116.

Chapter 5 - Finding the right provider

Hillcroft College is a women-only college. A one-year course leads to a Certificate in Higher Education; also offers a Diploma in Higher Education, and other courses. Contact: Hillcroft College, South Bank, Surbiton, Surrey KT6 6DF. Tel: 020 8399 2688. Website: www.hillcroft.ac.uk

Newbattle Abbey College offers 33-week courses leading to Diplomas in European Studies or Social Studies, which are recognised for entry to universities and higher education colleges across the UK. Short courses are also offered. Contact: Newbattle Abbey College, Newbattle Road, Dalkeith, Midlothian EH22 3LL. Tel: 0131 663 1921.

Northern College's programme includes a full-time nine-month diploma course (part-time study also possible), which is recognised as a university entrance qualification. The College also offers the first year of the Sheffield Hallam University degree course in Combined Studies. Various short courses are also available. Contact: Northern College, Wentworth Castle, Stainborough, Barnsley S75 3ET. Tel: 01226 776000. Website: www.northern.ac.uk

Plater College is a Catholic institution, but welcomes applications from people of other faiths. It runs a one-year Certificate in Higher Education, equivalent to the first year of a degree course. Students follow one of five subject pathway options. Contact: Plater College, Pullens Lane, Oxford OX3 0DT. Tel: 01865 740500. Website: www.plater.ac.uk

Ruskin College offers a Certificate of Higher Education, in a variety of subjects. Other courses include a Certificate of Higher Education in Community and Youth Work, Diploma of Social Work and Diploma of Higher Education in Social Change. Contact: Ruskin College Oxford OXI 2HE. Tel: 01865 310713. Website: www.ruskin.ac.uk

Other residential colleges

There are various other short-term residential colleges, offering mainly short leisure courses, in a wide field of subjects, such as in arts and crafts, music, history, natural history etc. For more information, see the publications by NIACE, listed below.

For more information about the adult residential colleges, contact the colleges direct for prospectuses, or view their websites.

Time to Learn – lists residential courses in the UK and overseas. Published annually by NIACE, 21 De Montfort Street, Leicester LE1 7EG. Tel: 0116 204 4269. Price £4.95 including postage and packaging.

The Adult Learning Year Book – also published by NIACE, includes lists of short-term residential colleges and community education centres. Price £16.95 and 10% postage and packaging.

Rebecca Malins – from an Access course onto a degree

'Having left school without completing my A levels, my ambition to become a teacher seemed out of reach. Becoming a mother made my dream appear even more unobtainable, until I began an Access course at the local college. Now, less than a year later, I have been offered a place at university to study for a BA honours degree.

It was a bit of a shock when the first assignments were due in. Having not written an essay for years I found myself sitting up all night before the deadline, but thanks to some really good tutors that only happened the once. I soon learnt to balance my workload, making the most of the facilities that were available to me.

Information technology was a daunting prospect, and the first time I touched a keyboard I nearly crashed the system. However it wasn't long before I learnt what the hard drive was, and terms like website, formatting and downloading suddenly had a meaning to me.

Overall, this last year has been more than just a learning experience; I was surprised to find so many people in the same position as I was. Having expected to be surrounded by spotty teenagers with raging hormones it was reassuring to be working with people my own age. Even the college support network is geared towards helping the mature students; they even helped me arrange a childminder for when I'm attending lessons.

I never believed I could have got this far, but I have enjoyed every moment of it, and feel I am really achieving something. I am looking forward to the next three years at university and would highly recommend anyone to return to study, whatever their age.'

Chapter 5 - Finding the right provider

Universities and colleges of higher education

The higher education system has expanded rapidly in recent years. This expansion has included a significant increase in the numbers of mature students. The traditional image of a university as a place for young people attending full-time courses is now out-dated. Although there has been a small drop in the numbers of new mature applicants over the last year or so (attributed by some to the introduction of fees and phasing out of grants), if you are contemplating higher education, you will not be alone! What is more, plenty of support is available. Several of the profiles included within this book describe the experiences of those who have embarked on higher education as mature students, and show vividly the sense of satisfaction and achievement that they experience.

Nowadays, in many institutions, the proportion of mature undergraduates is surprisingly high. Most part-time students are mature, and up to a third or more of full-time undergraduates being mature is not unusual. However, this proportion does vary tremendously between different institutions, and some still have only a very small proportion of mature students. When looking at the spread of ages amongst mature students in higher education, nearly two thirds, as might be expected, are in their twenties, almost a third are in their thirties, with just a small proportion aged 40 or more. You will also find that mature students are not necessarily evenly spread amongst the different subject areas – typically, more are found on arts and social science courses than science and engineering courses, for example. The UCAS directory *University & College Entrance: The Official Guide*, cites the overall proportions of mature students on degree and HND courses within each institution. N.B. The precise definition of a mature student can vary, but for most purposes it is defined by higher education institutions as being 21 years of age or over on entry (20 and over in Scotland).

Along with an expansion of student numbers in recent years, there has also been an increase in the flexibility of courses. This has resulted in much more opportunity to study for a degree on a part-time basis, which is an attractive option to many mature students.

Universities and other higher education institutions are committed to a policy of widening access; all are prepared to consider, indeed welcome, mature applicants who lack the formal entry requirements. Many HE institutions have mature student societies, which. represent the interests of mature students, and provide a contact point for them. You will, of course, usually find crèche facilities available.

What courses are available?

The higher education sector is made up of universities and, perhaps less well known, colleges or institutes of higher education. All these institutions offer courses at 'higher education' level, i.e.:

- **degrees** – leading to BA, BSc, BEd, etc – usually three or four years' full-time, or longer part-time
- **HNDs (Higher National Diplomas)** – two-year full-time or three-year sandwich (i.e. with a period in industry in the middle) or HNCs (Higher National Certificates) which are normally part-time courses
- **Diplomas of Higher Education** (usually two years full-time) and Certificate of Higher Education (normally one-year full-time); such courses may also be offered on a part-time basis
- some **professional** qualifications
- **postgraduate** courses.

In addition, many HE institutions run short courses and programmes of adult and continuing education, which can provide a good introduction back into study. N.B. A more comprehensive explanation of the qualifications available at higher education level is given in Chapter four.

As has already been discussed, further education colleges also deliver higher education courses, so, besides researching what's on offer at your nearest universities and higher education colleges, check out what your local further education colleges offer. For example, FE colleges are major providers of HND and HNC courses.

Universities have the authority to award their own degrees. They also award degrees offered by colleges of higher education and degrees run at further education colleges. You will find that the degree courses run at your local college are usually awarded by a neighbouring university.

The range of courses offered by higher education institutions varies, for each institution has its own particular history, strengths and traditions. For example, some were formerly teacher training colleges, so teaching and the arts are a strength; others were polytechnics before 1992, so vocational courses are well represented, and strong links with industry may be a feature. Some institutions offer specialist vocational courses which reflect particular industries of the region, developed through links with local companies.

Chapter 5 - Finding the right provider

Flexibility of learning

In recent years, there has been a strong move towards modular or unit-based courses – as described in chapter three. This has led to a greater choice in study options - in many courses, for example, you choose your modules as you progress, gradually shaping your course and building up towards your qualification over time. Modularisation of courses also means that it is easier to offer a part-time route to qualification, as students can build up modules at a pace that suits them. Furthermore, all is not lost if you need to take a break from your course for a period (although, of course, you would need to check out the financial and other implications of such a decision very carefully).

Some of the courses offered by universities are available through distance learning packages.

Finding the information

A glance at a higher education course directory or university prospectus will tell you that higher education institutions offer a huge range of courses; Manchester Metropolitan University, for example, offers over 500 courses in 130 different subject areas. For ease of reference, most institutions publish a number of guides for prospective students. To find out more about the courses that interest you, it is important to get hold of the right publications. These may include all, or some, of the following:

- **undergraduate prospectus** – full-time (and sandwich) degrees and diplomas
- **part-time prospectus** – which may include short courses
- **postgraduate prospectus** – including both taught masters and research degrees
- **extra-mural studies information** – adult education courses open to the general public
- **course/departmental booklets** – describing individual courses in more depth
- **professional and industrial training portfolio** – short courses for those at work
- **mature students' guide** – advice and information for prospective mature students.

Coming Back to Learning

And if you want to speak to someone personally, admissions officers, course tutors and student advisers may be able to give you much more detailed advice and assistance. Do not hesitate to seek such advice; providing it is part of the role of these staff, and it is in everyone's interests that you make the right decision about entry.

When considering higher education, bear in mind:

> - the choice of qualifications on offer - remember there are courses other than degrees
> - the variation of lengths of courses
> - the availability of courses on a part-time, or perhaps a distance learning, basis
> - the need for self-discipline and motivation - a considerable amount of private research and background reading is expected when following courses at this level.

Most applications for full-time higher education courses are handled by UCAS - the Universities and Colleges Admissions Service. Information about applying through UCAS, together with information about the other applications clearing houses, is described in chapter eight.

Don't get put off if you don't have the stated entry qualifications.........

Remember that course entry requirements may be relaxed for mature students. Course admissions tutors are mainly interested in whether you have the ability to cope with the course. They will therefore be looking at your experience and any other qualifications you have taken. They may also want to know whether you have undertaken any recent study. If they have concerns that you may not be ready for a particular course, they will advise on some preparatory learning that you could do first.

Postgraduate study

There are a huge range of postgraduate courses available; the various awards are described on page 63. Some are taught courses, others are higher degrees offered after undertaking research. Some are vocational, whilst others are academic. While many students follow a full-time programme, many more postgraduate students study part-time. Some are available on a distance-learning basis.

Chapter 5 - Finding the right provider

For more information on the courses provided through universities and higher education colleges, consult some of the directories and reference books listed below. Many will be available for reference in careers centre libraries, and through adult information, advice and guidance agencies; some may also be available in public reference libraries. Agencies may also provide access to computer databases such as *ECCTIS UK Course Discover*, to help you identify possible courses.

UCAS – Rosehill, New Barn Lane, Cheltenham GL52 3LZ. Tel: 01242 227788. A huge amount of information, including a course search facility, is available on their website: www.ucas.com

The Mature Student's Guide to Higher Education – available free of charge from UCAS. Essential reading for any prospective mature student. Available from the UCAS Distribution Team. Tel: 01242 544610.

University and College Entrance: The Official Guide – annually published by UCAS, this directory lists all full-time and sandwich higher education courses across the UK. Contains, for each institution, proportion of mature students.

The Laser Compendium of Higher Education – annually published directory, from Butterworth-Heinemann.

Going for Higher Education: a guide to moving on, moving up with better qualifications – published by How To Books, £12.95.

The NATFHE Handbook of Initial Teacher Training in England and Wales – details the full range of undergraduate and postgraduate teacher training courses. Published annually by NATFHE, 27 Britannia Street, London WC1X 9JP.

CRAC Degree Course Guides – published by Hobsons, covers over 30 subject areas. Includes information about who offers the courses, the differences and similarities between courses and graduate outlook.

The Complete Guides Series 2001 – a series covering seven subject areas at higher education level; each includes course characteristics and career prospects. Published by UCAS in association with Trotman.

The PUSH Guide to Which University – published by Letts Educational. 2000 edition, £12.99. Available through Trotman.

How to Choose Your Postgraduate Course – published by Trotman, £11.99.

The Open University

The Open University is the largest single provider of distance education in the UK. It has an international reputation for providing higher education to adults. Many courses do not require any formal academic qualifications for entry. Though best known for its range of courses leading to first degrees, the Open University offers a variety of programmes. These include:

> general BA or BSc degrees, in the arts and sciences, and degrees in particular subject areas
> professional diplomas in areas such as health and social welfare, education and management development programmes through the Open Business School
> postgraduate awards such as masters degrees in education and business and other areas
> courses and study packs in arts, education, social sciences, computing, technology and management.

The Open University's courses are open to anybody over 18 years of age. There are no entry requirements for the undergraduate degree programmes. They are genuinely open: there are no admission interviews or other formalities, and if you apply early enough then you will get a place. For postgraduate degrees, you will usually need an honours degree (or equivalent qualification).

First degrees

Undergraduate programmes are organised into a series of separate courses, each worth a particular number of credit points - usually 30 or 60. A 30-point course means at least seven hours of study a week; 14 hours a week for a 60-point course, spread over a year. You need 360 points to get a degree. There is no limit on the amount of time you can take to get a degree.

There is a wide range of subject areas on offer, covering the arts, social sciences, maths, science and technology. If aiming at a general degree, you choose the topics to cover as you go along. If you wish to gain a named subject degree, such as Business Studies, History, Law or Psychology, most of your study must be within a specified range of courses.

Students are sent course materials by post; this includes printed textbooks and workbooks, and other resources such as special equipment, audio and video cassettes or computer software. Completed assignments are sent back to tutors to be marked. Some courses include radio and television broadcasts, and many courses have one-week residential summer schools. Most importantly, support from tutors is provided, by phone, postal correspondence and e-mail. Support may also include tutorial meetings of students at a local study centre. Students are assessed through marked assignments and written examinations, held at a local centre.

The cost of a 60-point course varies, but is generally £390, or around £660 if it includes a week's residential school. The University has a limited Financial Awards Fund, to provide some help for students who would otherwise find it difficult to pay the fees. The OU can advise further.

It can take six years or more to gain a degree. You can get credit for any previous study in higher education, which would reduce the number of courses you need to do. For most students, however, gaining an Open University degree is a long haul - but thousands do it!

Non-degree courses

You do not have to register for a degree or diploma-level qualification to study with the Open University. As most courses within the degree programme are free-standing, you can choose to study an individual course if you wish.

There are also, as mentioned previously, a range of other courses available. Some of these are work-related, other study packs, relating to cultural education, the arts and history of ideas, for example, are for personal interest.

The OU also offers return to study packs.

Applying

You can apply for Open University courses at any time. Degree courses run over a calendar year from February to November; applications for degrees should be in by the end of October of the preceding year. As the number of places available on some courses is limited - and it's first come, first served - for the most popular programmes (such as those in the arts) you would need to apply early.

You can get further information about all courses, and information on fees and financial support from any of the OU's 13 regional centres. Information (including a list of centres) is also available on the OU website: www.open.ac.uk

For general enquiries, or as a starting point, contact:

The Central Enquiry Service – PO Box 724, The Open University, Walton Hall, Milton Keynes MK7 6ZS. Tel: 01908 653231.

The regional centres include the following:

The Open University in Wales – 24 Cathedral Road, Cardiff CF1 9SA. Tel: 029 2066 5636.

The Open University in Scotland –10 Drumsheugh Gardens, Edinburgh EH3 7QJ. Tel: 0131 225 2889.

The Open University in Ireland – 40 University Road, Belfast BT7 I SU. Tel: 028 9024 5025.

Courses, Diplomas and BA/BSc Degrees – annually updated brochure on OU courses, available from the Central Enquiry Service. This is one of a series of publications describing the various programmes of study. Includes some information about help with fees.

Independent providers

There is a variety of independent providers of learning opportunities, operating outside the public sector, offering both academic and vocational courses to the public.

> - Some providers run on purely commercial lines, others are registered educational charities.
> - Some run courses which require attendance at the college/training centre for teaching sessions, others offer distance learning (correspondence), with full tutor back up.
> - Courses on offer include GCSE and A level courses and a very wide range of professional and vocational qualifications, such as business studies, computing, accountancy, beauty therapy or secretarial qualifications.
> - Some of the larger organisations offer a wide range of courses; other smaller providers deliver courses related to a specific occupational area – ranging from photography to business skills, or concentrating on academic qualifications.

Apart from a few larger organisations, most independent providers are smaller than publicly-funded institutions. Many are found in London and the major cities, although you are likely to find some, in particular private colleges running secretarial/office skills courses, based in larger towns. Of course, location of institutions offering distance learning courses is immaterial, as they can cater for students from any geographical area.

Standards and accreditation

Standards in the private sector vary and, in general, course fees are higher than in the public sector, but the best colleges offer a good alternative route for adults to gain qualifications. If wanting to take a course which you hope will help you in your career, you should **check that the qualifications offered are nationally recognised**.

Accreditation by one of the bodies listed below assures you that the college meets certain quality standards. However, you will find that many colleges are not accredited (there is no legal requirement for accreditation). They offer courses in all sorts of subjects from photography to languages, and many run good quality courses which offer value for money, although there is no easy way of knowing. You could try to contact former students and seek their views. Most importantly, asking pertinent questions of admissions staff should help give you the information you need.

Ask about:

- the success rates of previous students
- the amount of tutor contact you should expect
- their range of facilities
- how long they have been established
- the credentials of staff
- what organisations they are members of or accredited through.

Many independent colleges are accredited through the **British Accreditation Council for Independent Further and Higher Education** (usually abbreviated to BAC). Accredited Colleges are required to receive an inspection every five years, and may have interim visits. N.B. Colleges that advertise themselves as members of the Conference for Independent Further Education (CIFE) are BAC accredited.

Organisations providing distance education and correspondence courses are accredited through the **Open and Distance Learning Quality Council** (ODL QC). The Council can supply lists of accredited colleges.

The following are some well-known providers of distance learning in the independent sector:

The National Extension College (NEC)

The NEC is a registered independent educational charity, which has been in operation over 30 years. It provides over 140 home study courses, both academic and vocational. Courses range from those you can do purely for pleasure, or those that help you to return to learning, through to professional-level courses in a variety of fields. Courses include GCSEs, A levels and degree courses, and a variety of courses in business skills, counselling, art and design and creative writing. Students work through learning packages at a time and pace to suit themselves. You are assigned a personal tutor, who you may have contact with by phone, post, or e-mail. Enrolments can be taken at any time of the year. Contact: Student Advisers, National Extension College, 18 Brooklands Avenue, Cambridge CB2 2HN. Tel: 01223 450200. Website: www.nec.ac.uk

The Open College of the Arts (OCA)

The OCA is a charitable trust, offering home study courses in a wide range of subject areas related to the arts, such as art and design, interior design, photography, creative writing and music. No previous experience is necessary. It is possible through your studies to gain credit towards higher education qualifications. Contact: Open College of the Arts, Houndhill, Worsbrough, Barnsley S70 6TU. Tel: 01226 730495 or freephone 0800 731 2116. Website: www.oca-uk.com

There are a number of resources and organisations you can consult to find out more about the opportunities within the independent sector:

Independent Colleges: a directory of courses – lists over 600 institutions. Includes full-time, part-time and distance learning opportunities. Published by ISCO publications, £6.50.

Distance & Supported Open Learning – containing over 4,500 courses, this annually updated reference directory covers the UK and

Chapter 5 - Finding the right provider

worldwide. Published by Hobsons, £36.99. May be available in reference libraries.

The OFL-CD – a comprehensive database of open, flexible and resource-based learning. Developed for the DfEE and learndirect, this database may be available at adult guidance agencies.

BAC – British Accreditation Council for Independent Further and Higher Education – Westminster Central Hall, Storey's Gate, London SW1H 9NH. Tel: 020 7233 3468. Their website lists approximately 100 colleges that have been accredited and inspected: www.the-bac.org

ODL QC – Westminster Central Hall, Storey's Gate, London SW1H 9NA. Tel: 020 7233 3468. A list of accredited colleges is available on their website: www.odlqc.org.uk

Association of British Correspondence Colleges (ABCC) – PO Box 17926, London SW19 3WB. Tel: 020 8544 9559. The Association consists of over 20 colleges, who comply with the Association's Code of Ethics. Website: www.homestudy.org.uk

Study and training abroad

There are opportunities for study and training abroad; particularly within the European Union. Education and training in EU member states is available to UK citizens on the same terms as citizens of that country. Obviously, courses will normally be taught in the language of the host country, so you would need to be sufficiently fluent to cope. There are, of course, many language schools abroad, which offer short intensive courses. Most advertise in the national press.

Higher education abroad: there are opportunities to study for up to a year abroad as part of your UK-based degree course; for some courses, the year abroad forms an integral part of the course. You can also spend from three months to a year abroad as part of your higher education course through the EU's Socrates-Erasmus programme. This programme covers EU and EEA (European Economic Area) countries, Cyprus and some Central and Eastern European Countries. Details of study abroad possibilities are provided in some higher education directories and within prospectuses. Further afield, universities and colleges worldwide are keen to attract overseas students. However, fees are likely to be high for overseas students. Contact the Embassy of the country of interest to you, to find out the possibilities.

UK Socrates-Erasmus Council – Research and Development Building, University of Kent, Canterbury CT2 7PD. Tel: 01227 762712. Publishes booklet on the Erasmus scheme *Information for Students*. See also the website: www.ukc.ac.uk/ERASMUS/erasmus

Vocational training: training in EU states is, in theory, open to all. There is an EU programme, Leonardo da Vinci, which offers work placements in companies in European countries, primarily aimed at young trainees and workers, and students on vocational higher education courses. The area covered is similar to the Erasmus programme described above. Training elsewhere in the world is hard to come by, as most countries only accept immigrants who have skills and qualifications to offer.

Leonardo da Vinci programme – The Central Bureau for Educational Visits and Exchanges, 10 Spring Gardens, London SW1A 2BN. Tel: 020 7389 4064. Website: www.leonardo.org.uk

Many careers centres and guidance agencies stock *Eurofacts* and *Globalfacts* leaflets, factsheets which include information about study in European and certain English speaking countries worldwide. The following are also useful.

One in Europe 2000 – a guide to working, studying or taking time out in Europe, Australia, New Zealand, Canada and the USA. Published by DfEE in association with Radio 1. Tel: 0845 602 2260 for a free copy.

Study Abroad – published annually by UNESCO. 2000 edition £17.50 plus postage. Available from The Stationery Office, Publications Centre, PO Box 206, London SW8 5DT.

And finally…..

All learning providers have staff whose role it is to provide information and advice. Some have advisers especially to help adults enquirers. Besides talking to general admissions advisers, you may have specific questions that only the course tutor can answer. Do not hesitate to ask any question you feel you need to know, and persist until you get an answer. In the long run, it is much better for both you and the provider that you should enrol on the right course; to do that, you need all the necessary information.

Chapter 5 - Finding the right provider

If you are uncertain about visiting a college, then ask a friend to accompany you for moral support. Many learning providers hold occasional open days (or evenings) for potential mature students. These provide an opportunity to talk informally with tutors. Though obviously restricted to a single institution, open days give you the chance to see some of the facilities and get a feel for the environment.

Coming Back to Learning

CHAPTER 6
Paying your way

> 'Of course getting into debt is a daunting prospect - but when you think about it, you're making a pretty safe investment, like taking out a mortgage only smaller.'

If you've followed the advice in the previous chapters, you've now got a pretty good idea of the course of education or training you wish to follow. So, it's time to look at the costs. All post-compulsory education and training comes with a price tag - even if it's only the loss of what you could be earning in the time you are learning! There are sources of funding for adults, but much of it is means-tested. So, before taking up a course or training place, you should work out what it is going to cost you in fees, books and equipment, transport, childcare and other expenses - and then find out what help is available in the form of loans, bursaries, concessions, sponsorship and so on.

What financial help is available depends on a number of factors - particularly the type and level of course you take, your personal circumstances - and which part of the UK you live and study in. Since Scotland, Northern Ireland and, to a lesser extent, Wales have all gained some degree of autonomy, student support is one area where their provision may differ from that in England. This chapter tries to include information where that difference is of note.

Some general points

Full-time education

Adults on full-time courses may be eligible for a variety of bursaries and loans. In higher education – that's Higher National Diplomas, degrees etc (see chapter four for a detailed definition) – the system of student loans and help towards tuition fees operates. For masters and research degrees, you may receive a postgraduate award. A possible source of funding for any job-related course – in both the independent and public sectors – is a Career Development Loan. Colleges and universities also have access funds which provide limited payments for full-time students facing hardship, and some government bursaries are available. All these payments and loans are welcome, but few are sufficient. Many full-time students (of all ages) are taking part-time jobs to make ends meet.

Part-time education, short courses and evening classes

There is some support for part-time students in higher education, but the general rule for part-time students in further education is that you are expected to support yourself. However, for those on income support or other state benefits, there are lower concessionary fees – or even a total fee waiver – for many part-time and short courses. Disabled student allowance is paid to students with disabilities on part-time courses. If your course is vocational, or at least job-related, then you might be able to obtain a Career Development Loan.

Benefit claimants

Full-time students are not usually eligible for benefits, though there are exceptions for single parents, students with disabilities, and student couples with dependant children. However, you may be able to study on a part-time course without losing benefit entitlement providing it meets certain rules about how much guided learning is involved; see page 120). If you have been unemployed for over six months (less in some cases), you become eligible for the Work-based Learning for Adults (WbLA) programme, which is designed to help people back to work through a mix of training and work experience. The New Deal includes education and training options. If you are on a Government-funded training scheme, obviously your fees are paid for you.

Chapter 6 - Paying your way

What's in this chapter

This chapter will help you to assess the costs you are likely to have to meet, and gives details of the main sources of financial help and support for adult learners. The chapter is organised under the following headings:

The costs
- course fees
- other study costs

The help available
- assistance with fees
- student loans
- special help for mature students/lone parents/students with disabilities
- access funds and hardship loans
- NHS bursaries
- payments to trainee teachers
- Dance and Drama Awards
- adult education bursaries
- sponsorships and scholarships
- postgraduate awards
- Career Development Loans
- individual learning accounts
- educational trusts and charities
- income support and other benefits
- government-funded training programmes
- trade unions
- part-time work
- employers.

Studying and training overseas

Sources of help and advice

Further information

The costs

Course fees

Higher education

Students on degree, DipHE, HND and other higher education courses (including the new two-year foundation degrees starting in 2001) may be asked to contribute to their tuition fees. The maximum contribution for 2000/2001 is £1050 per year. This is means-tested, and is reviewed each year. The amount of your contribution will depend on your own income or, depending on your circumstances, that of your parents or your husband or wife. 'Independent' students - those who are aged 25 or over before the start of the academic year, or married for at least two years before the start of the academic year, or who have supported themselves for at least three years before the start of the academic year - do not have parents' income taken into account.

> Tuition fee payments are made directly to the university or college when required.

> Scottish students attending HE institutions in Scotland do not have to pay tuition fees in advance, but most of those entering HE from 2001 will be expected to pay £2000 towards their fees into a new Graduate Endowment fund once they are earning over £10,000. Mature students, lone parents and students with disabilities need not pay this.

> At the time of writing the situation in Northern Ireland is similar to England and Wales, but the Northern Ireland Assembly is debating the whole issue of student support.

For students who pay their own fees in full, for instance because they do not meet the residence eligibility criteria or have received financial help for a previous course, universities set their own rates. These can be several thousands of pounds.

> *'It may sound silly, but managing on a pittance can actually be quite fun when you know it's only temporary. Cooking a gourmet dinner for four on a budget of, say, a fiver gives you a warm glow of accomplishment! You become expert on when and where to pick up the bargains in each supermarket.'*

Further education

In England, Wales and Northern Ireland anyone aged 19 or over may have to pay fees for further education. In Scotland, all full-time FE fees have been abolished; fees are only payable by students aged 18 or over on part-time courses. Where fees are applicable, most further education colleges have a flexible fee structure for their courses with a range of concessions for those on benefits or very low incomes. Most quote fees on an annual basis, though some allow you to pay in instalments over the year. Annual full-rate fees for full-time academic and vocational courses range from about £500 to £700. For example, fees for full-time Access courses are around £600 to £700. Annual fees for part-time day-release courses range from £300 to £500+, though often with substantial reductions for benefit claimants. 'Drop-in' centres for computing, office skills etc charge by the hour, usually between £3 to £4. For an evening course - for example an AS level taught one evening a week over the academic year - expect a fee of around £60 to £100. Do check with the education provider concerned for exact costs. Even in the public sector, colleges and adult education centres have considerable discretion over what they charge self-financing students. Some colleges choose to charge a nominal fee only for adults on full-time courses; it's well worth 'shopping around' colleges within your reach. Private education and training providers charge what they feel the market will bear; voluntary organisations are likely to set fees to just cover costs. In general, fees will vary according to the length of course, the particular education provider and the type of course; with those involving special equipment, laboratory or workshop facilities usually costing more.

For recreational education, expect to pay between £2 and £4 per hour. So, for a two-hour course over ten weeks, fees range between £40 and £80, or about £150 to £250 per academic year. Fees are usually payable either each term or at the outset of the course.

Open and distance learning

Correspondence courses and open or distance learning packages, while very convenient for those who can only study at home, are not cheap. Prices vary enormously depending upon the type of package, the amount of support material provided and the quality of tutorial support and back up. The following (2000) prices give some idea of fee levels.

The National Extension College charges £255 for a GCSE course, with £200 for each additional GCSE on the same enrolment, and £295 for an A level course, again lowering to £225 for additional A levels.

Open University fees vary from course to course. Just as an example, you would pay £390 in tuition fees for a Level 1 science course, worth 60 points towards a 360 point bachelor's degree, plus £260 for the residential school fee. Most OU students undertake to gain 60 points in one year of part-time study. Fees can be paid in instalments.

Prices for courses with the Open College of the Arts range from £255 to £409.

Details you should check

In general, if you are paying you own fees for any type of course, then check the following:

- **hidden charges**: on some courses there are extra charges for registration, examination and assessment fees, supplements for use of specialist equipment and (returnable) breakages deposits; so find out if the fee is inclusive or whether there are hidden extras.

- **concessionary fees**: colleges and education centres have individual policies on charging reduced fees for those on benefits or low incomes. You need to check whether you are eligible for a concessionary fee and the level of reduction.

- **instalments**: paying by instalments may be an option. If it would suit you, ask whether payments can be staggered.

- **cancellations**: it's worth while reading the small print to find out what you might lose if you have to withdraw before starting a course or during its early stages.

Other study costs

Expenses like books, travel and perhaps childcare costs have to be accounted for as well as course fees. You need to consider the cost of:

- books and equipment
- examination fees and other charges
- field trips

Chapter 6 - Paying your way

> transport costs
> childcare costs
> costs of caring for other dependant relatives
> living expenses, especially if you have to run a second home.

Whatever your course and your personal circumstances, you are bound to incur some or all of these costs. Many students - including school-leavers - are cutting costs by studying close to home. Is this a possibility in your case? The issue of childcare provision is covered in chapter eight.

The university or college you are applying to can give you some idea of the likely costs of books, equipment and other fees. It is easy to underestimate the costs of books; you cannot always rely on libraries. It is often possible to buy second-hand - either from shops or from students a year ahead of you. There are likely to be charges for photocopying and printing, for accommodation on field trips and for special materials and equipment for practical courses.

Another aspect to consider is the 'opportunity cost' of studying, that is the amount that you could be earning were you working instead of studying. If you give up a job to return to education, then you need to assess whether you believe it is worth the loss of income. But mature students rarely regret returning to education. They might be poorer for it in the short term but many come to value the investment in time and money.

> *'I expect I moaned about how hard up I was while I was on the course, but looking back, it was well worth the struggle. I can earn far more money now and in the future than I ever would have done without my qualification - and I get more job satisfaction than I used to.'*

The help available

Assistance with fees

Higher education

For married independent students, the husband or wife is expected to make a contribution to tuition fees, and possibly living costs, if their residual income (that's the income remaining after the deduction of certain allowances from gross income) is over £15,070 a year. There is a sliding scale of increasing contributions.

Because of these arrangements, most students pay less than the maximum tuition fee contribution, and about a third of students don't have to pay any contribution towards their fees at all.

Part-time students on benefits or on a low income may apply to have their tuition fees waived. You should apply to the college or university if you think you may be eligible.

To qualify for financial assistance, higher education students normally must have been 'ordinarily resident' in the British Islands for the three years before the start of the academic year in which the course begins. If you have previously undertaken higher education with assistance from public funds, your entitlement to help with tuition fees may be affected.

> All students, even if they think they will have to pay the maximum student tuition fee, must apply to their local education authority for assessment.

Further education

Most further education providers have a policy of giving concessions or waiving fees for those on benefits or low incomes. Basic literacy and numeracy courses are usually free. Some adult education centres, which are run by local authorities, have a policy of charging more for those who attend from outside that authority. All full-time and some part-time Scottish FE students do not have to pay fees.

The Open University

The OU has its own limited funding to assist less well off students, i.e. those on benefits or low incomes. A leaflet on financial support for OU students is available from OU regional centres.

Student loans

The main source of funding for living costs for students on full-time courses is a student loan. Around three quarters of the maximum loan will be available to all students under the age of 50, and to those aged 50-54 who intend to return to work after studying. How much of the remaining quarter of the loan you can claim will depend on your income, and/or that of your family. Your LEA will confirm the amount of loan you are entitled to at the same time that they assess your contribution towards tuition fees. You then

Chapter 6 - Paying your way

tell the Student Loans Company how much of the loan you want, and they will pay it to you. The maximum loan available for a student living away from home, and not studying in London, is £3725, or if living at home is £2950 (slightly less for the final year). Scotland is considering removing the cap on parents' earnings, so that the most well-to-do are expected to fully support their student offspring, although a minimal amount of loan would still be made available to the student.

Repaying the loan

> From the April after students have finished or left their course, if their income rises above a threshold of £10,000, they will begin to repay the loan at an interest rate linked to inflation. If their income falls below the threshold level his or her repayments will be suspended.

> For most borrowers, repayments will be collected by their employer. If you are self-employed, you will repay the loan through the tax self-assessment system.

> There is no fixed time limit for repayment. Any outstanding loan will be cancelled when you reach the age of 65, or if you become permanently disabled or you die.

> Full details of the loan system are sent to prospective students by their LEA.

N.B. For the first four years of a medicine or dentistry course, the financial arrangements described above apply. For year five and beyond, funding will be through non-repayable bursaries, assessed against family income. For professions allied to medicine, see the section about NHS bursaries on page 113.

Part-time students:

Loans of up to £500 a year are available to some part-time students on low incomes, if they are studying the equivalent of 50% of a full-time course.

Special help for mature students/lone parents/ students with disabilities etc

Mature students on full-time higher education courses in England and Wales are eligible for a means-tested annual bursary of up to £1000 from autumn 2000, primarily to cover childcare and travel costs, as well as income-assessed grants towards children's school meals and an increased level of disregarded income (from £820 to £7500) for student support assessment. In Scotland, mature students entering HE for the first time can claim the full student loan and apply for assistance from the Mature Students' Bursary Fund. In Scotland, extra funding is being made available to assist with childcare costs for part-time FE students.

Some students are entitled to a supplementary grant for help in meeting certain living costs:

- students with dependants, including lone parents
- students with disabilities (Disabled Student Allowances)
- students who have previously been in care
- students who incur certain extra travel costs.

Grants for students with dependants are means tested. Dependants can include husband/wife, children and other adults, if they are financially dependent on you. Any income of your dependants is also taken into account when deciding your eligibility.

Disabled Student Allowances (DSAs), which are paid through your local education authority, are not means-tested. The DSAs are intended to cover any extra costs you have as a student because of your disability e.g. for specialist equipment and non-medical helpers, such as sign language interpreters. They are not intended to meet costs which you would still incur if you were not a student. Your LEA or the DfEE (tel: 0800 731 9133) can provide a leaflet called *Bridging the Gap*.

Students who have previously been in care can get a grant of up to £100 a week to help with accommodation costs in the long vacation. The LEA can tell you more about eligibility.

Students with a disability or students who have certain exceptional travel costs, including having to travel outside the UK as part of the course, can claim assistance after the first £255.

Access funds and hardship loans

Hardship loans and access funds are available mainly to help students who have difficulties meeting their living costs, including childcare and transport. Access funds are allocated annually to colleges and universities. They allow for payments (not loans) to students who have serious financial difficulties or who might not otherwise have been able to afford to enter further or higher education. Each institution is free to determine its own priorities, deciding which students qualify and setting limits on payments. Some colleges have also set up their own hardship funds to help students in financial difficulties.

Unlike student loans, access funds are available to both students in further education (aged 19 and over) and to postgraduates. There is the same residence requirement, but otherwise all students on full-time, sandwich or part-time courses (if at least 50% of a full-time course) may apply for assistance. However, these funds are limited and may be insufficient to meet all demands.

Students must meet certain criteria and show that they have explored all other sources of finance.

Hardship loans of up to £500 per year are available to new entrants in serious financial difficulty, at the discretion of the college or university. Claimants must be eligible, and have applied, for a full student loan. The loan is added to the student loan for repayment.

Students should apply to the student services office of their institution for more information about each of these schemes.

NHS bursaries

The NHS funds students on a range of courses. NHS-funded places are available on pre-registration courses in physiotherapy, occupational therapy, orthoptics, radiography, nursing and midwifery degrees, speech and language therapy, chiropody, dietetics, dental hygiene, dental therapy, prosthetics and orthotics.

Financial assistance comprises course fees paid by the NHS, a means-tested bursary and access to student loans.

Students undertaking nursing and midwifery diploma courses (as opposed to degrees) receive a non-means-tested bursary, but are not eligible for student loans.

N.B. Not all places are NHS-funded. Students who do not receive NHS funds have the same entitlements to loans and help with tuition fees as other higher education students.

Payments to trainee teachers

Because of the fall in recruits to teacher training over recent years, various 'golden hello' schemes have been tried to attract more students. From September 2000, students on full- and part-time postgraduate initial teacher training courses in England are paid a salary of £6000 per year during training. Those training to teach shortage subjects in secondary schools (maths, science, design and technology, information technology and modern languages) will receive a further £4000 on starting their second year of teaching. Arrangements for Wales are slightly different: trainees in non-shortage subjects will receive £4000 initially, plus a further £2000 on completion of one year's teaching, and the payment is called a training and teaching grant rather than a salary. Shortage subjects in Wales also include Welsh.

Mature entrants to teaching may be interested in employment-based training, through school-centred consortia, Graduate and Registered Teacher Programmes. These schemes involve being paid a salary as an unqualified teacher while receiving much of your training in school.

Undergraduate and postgraduate trainee teachers, and those on employment-based routes, can apply for the 'fast track' scheme, which carries a bursary of £5000. Successful students will start on a higher point on the salary scale than most, and be expected to climb to the top quickly through excellent teaching performance. Fast track teachers will receive extra support and continuing professional development. Eligibility depends on subject knowledge, communication skills, commitment and potential.

Undergraduate trainees in secondary shortage subjects may also be eligible for financial help, based on need, from the Secondary Shortage Subject Scheme in England or the Priority Subject Recruitment Initiative in Wales.

Chapter 6 - Paying your way

Dance and Drama Awards

A Dance and Drama Awards Scheme assists students on certain dance, drama and stage management courses, which offer recognised qualifications, at a number of independent colleges. These awards provide help with fees and maintenance (living costs) for over 800 students to enter training each year. Students audition for funded places. Successful students will not pay more than £1050 per year towards the cost of their fees. Students on higher and further education courses in dance and drama in the public sector have access to the same funding arrangements as students of other subjects. Further information is available from the dance and drama schools, or by telephoning 0114 259 3617 for a DfEE booklet.

Adult education bursaries

Students accepted on to a course at one of the eight UK long-term adult residential colleges (described in chapter five) may be eligible for an adult education bursary consisting of:

> tuition fees up to £976 (2000 figure)

> a means-tested maintenance grant of between £2235 and £3749, according to where the course is and whether you live at the college or in the parental home. The student's own income, husband's or wife's residual income if over £14,700, or parents' residual income if over £17,370 (if not of independent student status), will reduce the amount of grant received

> approved travel expenses of over £80 per year (the first £80 is included in the maintenance grant).

In addition, there are dependants' grants and two homes grants. Students with disabilities may be entitled to Disabled Students' Allowance.

Sponsorships and scholarships

Some employers and other organisations sponsor degree and HND students, mostly on vocational courses related to science and engineering, and also for business-related courses. Sponsorship for arts courses is rare. If you obtain such funding, unless it is very generous, it should not affect your entitlement to assistance from

115

public funds. Unfortunately, mature students may find that young applicants are usually preferred.

Scholarships are provided by various bodies, offering extra financial assistance to students, usually on vocational courses. Individual colleges and universities may have scholarship funds at their disposal - not usually huge sums - to allocate to their students.

Postgraduate awards

Most of the available funding for postgraduate education and training comes from public bodies such as the six government-funded Research Councils and some government departments. Who funds what depends on the subject area. For instance, while the Medical Research Council funds study in the biomedical field, the Economic and Social Research Council funds areas such as economics, business studies and social administration, while conservation studies are supported by the Natural Environment Research Council. Support for arts and humanities courses is available through the Arts and Humanities Research Board and the British Academy.

Such awards are very limited. They are usually made on a competitive basis through the university or college concerned.

You will need to take time, care and trouble over the presentation of your application. A minimum of an upper second class honours degree is usually required. Few local education authorities give any funding for postgraduate study, especially not if the applicant has been funded through a first degree. Many postgraduate courses are offered on a part-time basis - perhaps through distance learning - so that coursework and study may be fitted around paid employment. Most postgraduate students follow this route.

Some other possible sources of funding for postgraduates are:

- a Career Development Loan (see next page)
- the Business School Loan Scheme, operated by certain banks, which offers cheap loans to students on MBA courses.
- family members may offer the best rates of interest on a loan!
- paid research or teaching assistantships in universities, which may allow postgraduate study
- charities and trusts (see page 119)

Chapter 6 - Paying your way

> scholarships and bursaries for research offered by universities, with money from contractual work for industry and commerce, or from university trust funds or access funds.

University careers offices will be able to advise you. Note that most will help any graduate, not just those from their own institution, so you can go to your local university for convenience.

Northern Ireland has a similar system, with the two universities organising the competition for awards, funded by Research Councils and administered by the Department of Higher and Further Education. In Scotland, postgraduate awards are allocated to certain courses by the Postgraduate Students' Allowances Scheme on a quota system. These are competed for in a similar way to the English system. Students on non-quota courses can also apply for assistance. This scheme is currently being reviewed.

Career Development Loans

Managed by the DfEE in partnership with four High Street banks, Career Development Loans are available to students and trainees on work-related education or training courses at all levels, both full-time and part-time, as well as distance learning programmes with providers like the Open University. The course must be vocational, and last for not more than two years (plus up to a year of work experience if it is part of the training). You can use the loan to pay for the last two years of a longer course. You are not entitled to a loan if you are receiving financial support for your training from other sources. You should intend to make use of your training by working in the UK or elsewhere in the EU or European Economic Area.

You can apply for a Career Development Loan to cover 80% of your course fees, plus the full costs of books, materials and other course costs, including, in some cases, living expenses. If you have been unemployed for more than three months, you can get a loan to cover 100% of your course fees provided your application is endorsed by your Training and Enterprise Council (TEC - Learning and Skills Councils from April 2001) or Local Enterprise Company (LEC). In most cases the largest loan you can receive is £8000 and you must borrow at least £300.

Career Development Loans are available from the Royal Bank of Scotland, Barclays, the Co-operative and the Clydesdale banks. They are fixed-rate loans set at interest rates prevailing when you apply. But they are attractive because the interest on the loan is paid for you by the DfEE during your training. You do not start to repay the loan until up to a month after completion of your course, over a period agreed with the bank. Repayment may be deferred for longer if you are unemployed and/or in receipt of benefits. This 'interest holiday' means that the loans are a cheaper source of finance than taking out a personal bank loan or running up an overdraft.

You can apply for a career development loan through one of the participating banks. They will check your credit rating and may refuse applications. An information pack and application form can be obtained by telephoning freephone 0800 585505.

Individual learning accounts

Individual learning accounts (ILAs) are available to workers aged 19 and over, but are targeted particularly at younger people with few qualifications, at women returners, self-employed people and non-teaching school staff. Initially, each account opened entitles the holder to £150 of government money - as long as the holder invests at least £25 of their own money - to pay towards education and training. Account holders also get a discount of 20% off the cost of accredited learning - 80% off certain courses. Employers will gain tax relief on contributions they make to their employees' learning accounts as an incentive for them to contribute to training. The scheme is operated by Capita Group - although Scottish Enterprise will run it in Scotland until Capita take over in 2001. Applicants can phone freephone 0800 072 5678 or find out more from website: www.dfee.gov.uk/ila

> *'After hearing about the pilot RSA Integrated Business Technology level 3 (IBT 3) course, I decided to open an ILA account and try my hand at this new course. I phoned the TEC to find out how to go about setting up an account, whether I was entitled to one and, if so, how much money they would give me! It turned out that they would pay £150 towards the cost of my chosen course, directly to the training provider, if I paid the first £25. Because I'm using the skills centre on a drop-in basis, the college only ask the TEC for £100, and if I pay for any exams up front I can get a claim form from the TEC and claim it all back. It couldn't have been easier. It's just one form with full instructions and a telephone number if you have any questions.*

If you haven't got an ILA yet, apply now. Don't miss out on money that – for the time being at least – is just sitting there waiting to be claimed.'

Educational trusts and charities

Numerous educational trusts and charities potentially provide an additional source of finance for students. However, these trusts should be seen very much as a last resort. Most will only assist students who have exhausted all other possible sources of financial support. But they do offer some, albeit limited, options for those who lack the funds to start a course and for those who run into unforeseen difficulties during a course.

Some general points to bear in mind

- Educational trust funds have strict terms of reference which they have to follow.
- Many funds are restricted to offering support for residents of a particular locality, such as a certain county, town or even parish.
- Some funds offer assistance only in relation to a specific area of study – such as agriculture, music or carpentry.
- Upper age limits are frequently cited, which can rule out prospective mature students.
- The amount of money payable is usually small.
- Often financial help is available only for expenditure on particular items - like books, travelling expenses or equipment.
- Assistance is not usually available for study at private institutions.
- Nationality is a criterion often mentioned in the terms of reference.
- Assistance may be in the form of a grant or a loan.

Sometimes, it is worth approaching the student support departments of local authorities for lists of educational trust funds. Certainly, seek information and advice from your local careers guidance service.

Once you have identified a fund that might be applicable to you, check carefully the terms of reference and closing dates for application. Apply to the trust fund as early as possible and, usually, about a year before you intend to commence your education or training course.

Income support and other benefits

Full-time students

The benefits system does not provide a safety net for most full-time students. In general, full-time students are not eligible for income support or housing/council tax benefit either in term-time or during vacations.

Some categories of full-time students may still be entitled to claim. The keyword is 'may': because of the complexity of benefit regulations and that individual claims need to be considered. You will need to get expert advice from the Benefits Agency, Employment Services' office, students' unions, local authority (for housing benefit) or Citizens Advice Bureaux. Those who may be able to claim one or more benefits include:

- single parents (including foster parents)
- students with disabilities
- refugees
- student couples with dependant children
- pensioner students
- OU students on summer school.

Part-time students

Part-time students who have been unemployed may be able to continue claiming Jobseekers Allowance, as long as the course they are on does not involve more than 16 hours of guided learning and they are prepared to leave the course if a suitable vacancy is found. A part-time student may also be eligible for housing/council tax benefit in certain circumstances.

Students - or couples where one member is a student - in receipt of Working Families'Tax Credit may continue to receive it as long as they can show they are in remunerative work for not less than 16 hours a week.

Please seek expert advice from the agencies mentioned above. Some information is available on website: www.dss.gov.uk/ba

Government-funded training programmes

There are a number of programmes for people who have been unemployed for some months which include education and training as an option - such as Work-based Learning for Adults and some New Deal provision. These programmes are described fully in chapter five. Participants will usually receive the equivalent of Jobseekers Allowance or other relevant benefits, plus £10 and, possibly a contribution to travel and other expenses. Course fees are paid on your behalf.

Trade unions

Trade unions have always been involved in providing education and training for their members. If you are a member of a trade union, you may be entitled to help through the General Federation of Trades Unions Education Trust. Since 1998, the Union Learning Fund has received government funding for projects, including the establishment of networks of learner representatives and lifelong learning advisers working in the workplace to advise members. Ask your union representative about both these sources of help.

Part-time work

Many students - including those on demanding full-time higher education courses - subsidise their education and training through working in the evenings or on tuition-free days. Universities and colleges often help students to find suitable part-time work with local firms; some even offer bar work, cleaning jobs, basic clerical work etc on-campus to students. Any work experience - especially for those who have not been in a work situation for some time - will help to improve key skills of teamwork, communication, problem solving and, perhaps, IT, however irrelevant the job may seem to your future career.

Employers

Finally, don't forget that employers have always been a significant sponsor of education and training. As direct government support for students is squeezed, they may be expected to share more of the burden. Some have signalled their readiness to invest further in the education and development of their employees through commitment to national initiatives like Investors in People, UfI learndirect and

Individual Learning Accounts. Some run their own employee development programmes, even to the extent of offering vocational degree courses in-house. Many postgraduate masters programmes rely heavily on industrial sponsorship, or, put another way, without employers paying fees and other expenses people simply would not be able to afford to attend. Whatever course you plan to take, if you are in employment, you should regard your employer as a potential source of assistance.

Siân Wiltshire – *learning while in a full-time job*

'I decided to go back to college and study for a certificate in applied animal behaviour as I eventually want to further my career as a veterinary nurse, and become a pet behaviourist. I finished training to become a veterinary nurse three years ago, and, although I enjoy the job, I felt as if I needed to have a new direction in my career. After a lot of thought, this was the path that I chose.

The course consists of eight, one-week modules, and is at degree-level standard. The modules are mainly theory-based. At the end of each week, we are set further work to be done at home - normally in the form of two 1500 to 2000-word essays.

The college is very supportive, as most of the students on the course are mature students. There is a mixture of ages, the youngest being about 19 and the oldest about 60. Not everyone on the course works with animals; there is also a hairdresser, a journalist and people in computers. The first module of the course was aimed at helping us learn about study techniques - writing essays, using the computer (including the Internet), and time management. It was all very easy to do in theory, but putting it into practice was a lot harder!

The rewarding part about returning to study is the fact that I'm really interested in the subject, so once I get into it I enjoy writing the essays. I have also made a lot new friends on the course. As most of us live far away, we all end up in the pub after each day at college!

The difficult part is making good use of time. With working full-time, trying to run the house and looking after all my animals, it is not always easy to find the time to do the research, reading and then the writing of the essays. It can also be very difficult to get motivated once I finish work. The other difficulty with the way the course is run, in weekly blocks, is getting the time off work. However, I'm lucky that my employer is very supportive and allows me to do the course in paid work time. Some of the other students have to use annual leave in order to complete the course. I do pay for the course, buy all the textbooks and pay for bed and breakfast, so each unit works out at about £300.

If you are in full-time employment and thinking of returning to studying, there are lots of things to consider. Are you able to find enough time to do any extra work that is needed to complete the course (there are normally deadlines)? If there is something you normally do, e.g. watching EastEnders, allow for this when doing a timetable. Arrange your study timetable with the whole household, and make sure people understand that when you are studying you are not to be disturbed. Training the dogs to understand this is the hard bit! It is important to enjoy the subject that you studying; it is impossible to get motivated and do well in a subject that you are not finding interesting.

I am thoroughly enjoying going to college and, after completing the certificate, I hope to go on and do a diploma in animal behaviour. From there on, who knows where it will lead?'

Studying and training overseas

There are a number of books and websites with information about funding for education and training overseas. Some assistance is available through European Union schemes designed to increase student exchanges within the EU. Socrates-Erasmus is a scheme which funds HE students who choose to spend part of their course in another EU country, and the Leonardo da Vinci programme encourages vocational training participation throughout Europe. Eurofacts and Globalfacts are information sheets, available for reference in many careers libraries, which include information on studying and training abroad.

Sources of help and advice

Nothing concerned with student finance is ever straightforward. Regulations covering tuition fees, loans and benefits change frequently. The rules are complex. For specific guidance, the best advice is to seek help from those who have up-to-date knowledge and those who control the purse strings. Consult your nearest adult educational and careers guidance service (see page 30) or the organisations listed below.

Colleges and universities

If you have been offered a place on a course then the college, university or education provider that runs the course should know about likely sources of finance and may be able to tell you how previous students have managed. Colleges are increasingly concerned about the financial plight of students and all offer advice and guidance. Usually, this help is available from student support offices or from welfare centres.

Some institutions have set up student financial aid and advice centres. Many also publish guides on budgeting and finance. The Open University, for example, produces a booklet giving a comprehensive listing of sources of help, grants and awards for its students. *Financial Support for Open University Study* may be obtained free of charge from the university's regional enquiry centres.

Students' unions are also an invaluable source of advice – especially where there are sections dedicated to mature students.

Local education authorities

Local education authorities are the first port of call to find out about your entitlement to help with tuition fees and access to student loans if you are undertaking a higher education course. A few authorities may offer help to other adult students, but generally speaking such financial support is now dealt with directly by colleges and universities.

TECs/LECs/Learning and Skills Councils

Training and Enterprise Councils (whose duties will be taken over in England by local Learning and Skills Councils from April 2001) may be able to offer a range of support. Responsible for the main government-sponsored schemes for unemployed adults (to transfer to Employment Services after April 2001), the Councils are currently able to support a number of initiatives in further and higher education at their own discretion. Some, for example, provide help with childcare for single parents and other groups of students. In Scotland, Scottish Enterprise's Local Enterprise Companies provide a similar range of services.

N.B. Some TECs are known as Chambers of Commerce, Training and Enterprise (CCTEs).

Citizens Advice Bureaux

Citizens Advice Bureaux staff are able to provide expert guidance on the benefits system and on dealing with financial problems. Offices will have information about sources of funding, including any local initiatives. They will also be able to refer you to other agencies that can provide support and assistance. The service is free and confidential.

Educational Grants Advisory Service

The Educational Grants Advisory Service (EGAS) – 501/505 Kingsland Road, London E8 4AU. Tel: 020 7254 6251.

EGAS is part of the Family Welfare Association which administers several educational trusts. It provides advice on student funding with particular emphasis on educational trusts and charities. EGAS is experienced in advising mature students and others returning to education – especially disadvantaged students such as lone parents, people with disabilities, asylum seekers and students on low incomes. You can either be referred by an EGAS member organisation, which includes many colleges, students' unions, local education authorities and careers services, or contact them direct by phone or by letter enclosing a stamped, self-addressed envelope.

> *'Money does not make the world go around; it just gives it a bit of a jump start.'*

For further information

Contact the student support section of your local education authority or, for Government-funded training, your TEC, LEC or Jobcentre.

Students in England and Wales can obtain:

Financial Support for Higher Education Students – free booklet on support in higher education, available from the DfEE's Student Support Information line. Tel: 0800 731 9133. Also on website: www.dfee.gov.uk

Financial Help in Further Education – free from DfEE Publications Centre, PO Box 5050, Annesley, Nottingham NG15 0DJ or by phoning 0845 602 2260.

Students resident in Scotland should contact the following for information about higher education funding:

Students Awards Agency for Scotland – Gyleview House, 3 Redheughs Rigg, South Gyle, Edinburgh EH12 9YT. Tel: 0131 476 8212. www.student-support-saas.gov.uk

For Scottish further education funding details, contact the college you wish to apply to, which should be able to advise you.

Students and trainees in Northern Ireland can contact the Awards Section of their regional Education and Library Board, their local Training and Employment Agency or:

Department of Higher and Further Education, Training and Employment for Northern Ireland – Adelaide House, 39/49 Adelaide Street, Belfast BT2 8FD. Tel: 028 9025 7777. Website: www.dhfeteni.gov.uk

Student Loans Company – enquiry line 0800 405 010.

Career Development Loans – FREEPOST, Newcastle upon Tyne NE85 1BR. Tel: 0800 585 505 between 8 am and 10 pm, Monday to Friday.

Financial Assistance for Students with Disabilities in Further Education and Training and *Financial Assistance for Students with Disabilities in Higher Education* – price £2 each from Skill, The Chapter House, 18-20 Crucifix Lane, London SE1 3JW. Tel: 0800 328 5050, or see: www.skill.org.uk

The Directory of Graduate Studies – published annually by CRAC/Hobsons. A comprehensive reference book covering over 20,000 opportunities for postgraduate study in the UK. Includes information on funding.

See also website: www.postgrad.hobsons.com

Directory of Grant-Making Trusts – published by the Charities Aid Foundation.

Guide to Postgraduate Studentships in the Humanities and *Guide to Postgraduate Professional and Vocational Awards* – both published by the Arts and Humanities Research Board, 10 Carlton House Terrace, London SW1Y 5AH. Tel: 0207 969 5205.www.ahrb.ac.uk

Chapter 6 - Paying your way

Prospects Postgraduate Funding Guide – published by CSU or available on their website: www.prospects.csu.ac.uk

Charities Digest – price £21.95 from Waterlow Legal Publishers, 6-14 Underwood Street, Old Street, London N1 7JQ. Tel: 020 7490 0049. Provides details and addresses of national and regional charities in the UK, including organisations which offer financial help to students and trainees.

The Grants Register – published by Macmillan Press Ltd. 18th edition price £99 – but may be available in your local reference library, Includes information on grants for further and higher education.

The Educational Grants Directory – published by the Directory of Social Change (available through Trotman). 2000 edition price approximately £19 (to be confirmed). A guide to the sources of funding available to students in need, listing trusts and foundations. Covers courses up to and including first degree level, but not postgraduate level.

Students' Money Matters – published by Trotman, £9.99.

University Scholarships and Awards – by Brian Heap, published by Trotman, £11.99.

Financial Help for Health Care Students – published by the NHS Executive and available for reference in careers centres.

Springboard Student Services: Sponsorship and Funding Directory – published annually by CRAC/Hobsons. 2000 edition priced at £8.99.

The Directory of Work and Study in Developing Countries – published by Vacation Work, £14.99.

Socrates-Erasmus: The UK guide for entry – published by the UK Socrates-Erasmus Council in association with ISCO, £12.50.

Study Abroad – published annually by UNESCO, £17.50.

Studying, Training and doing Research in another country of the European Union – free booklet published by the EU. Order by phoning 0800 581591.

Adult Education Bursaries: a guide for applicants for courses at the long-term residential colleges – is available from the Awards Officer, Adult Education Bursaries, c/o Ruskin College, Walton Street, Oxford OX1 2HE.

Dance and Drama Awards – a booklet should be available in careers libraries, or can be obtained from dance and drama colleges participating in the scheme.

Fulbright Commission Educational Advisory Service – Fulbright House, 62 Doughty Street, London WC1N 2JZ. Tel: 020 7404 6994. For information on funding for study in the US. Website: www.fulbright.co.uk

Information about **Socrates-Erasmus** and **Leonardo** is on website: http://europa.eu.int/citizens

A web guide to scholarships available can be found on website: www.freefund.co.uk

Information sheets on student finance are available from The Welfare Unit, National Union of Students, 461 Holloway Road, London N7 6LJ. Tel: 020 7272 8900. Send an A4 stamped, self-addressed envelope.

CHAPTER 7
Making your choice

So far this book has considered many aspects of learning, and provided information about the qualifications, possible providers, costs and so on. Sooner or later, the time comes when one has to make a decision about whether to embark on learning, and which opportunity to opt for.

In order to make a choice, you need to:

> - be clear about what you are aiming to achieve
> - identify all the relevant opportunities
> - find out as much as you can about them
> - then weigh up the pros and cons of each!

Work out your aims

In chapter two, possible reasons for a return to learning were considered. These reasons could include: for leisure or self development, to improve your work-related qualifications or to improve your academic qualifications – or perhaps a combination of all three! Even though you may not have worked out your long-term aims in detail, you should at least have a broad idea of your reasons for embarking on learning, and what you hope to achieve in the short term.

If your reasons for considering a return to learning relate to your future career plans, you will, of course, need to have decided on a career avenue – this need not be a specific job idea, but obviously you will need a broad career area in mind. Plenty of information about the qualification requirements of particular occupations can be found in reference books, databases and other careers resources, held in careers centres and adult guidance agencies. If you find yourself going round in circles when considering future career plans, these agencies can provide advice and guidance.

Take one step at a time

The most important point to underline is that you do not need to start out with a complete plan. Not everybody returning to learning has a clear idea about what they want to achieve ultimately, and most would admit to having doubts about what they are capable of achieving. People often underestimate their own abilities, and many end up studying at a level way above their initial expectations. But, once started, you also find that your ideas change, new interests develop and, as you gain confidence, you often find that one course leads naturally to another.

The most important thing is to decide on your starting point.

Build on your previous experience

As an adult-learner, you do not need to start at the bottom each time. You have two assets over school-leavers: maturity and experience. And, through working - indeed through living - you acquire skills and knowledge over and above those acquired through education. It is important to take these as your starting points.

Education and training organisations recognise that adults bring additional qualities and are not starting straight from school. As described in chapter four, through the process of APL or APEL, recognition for skills learnt outside a formal educational or training environment, as well as those acquired on other courses can sometimes be gained. Many admissions tutors are prepared to waive standard entry requirements if you have relevant work experience, though you may be asked to sit an aptitude test or take a preparatory course.

Identify all the relevant opportunities

Making good decisions requires having all the relevant information. In this respect, there is no substitute for getting detailed information from course organisers. But, course programmes and college prospectuses can only tell part of the story; they can seem daunting, presenting you with a complex selection of choices and options. So how do you find out what courses are really like?

There are two practical steps you can take. The first is to talk to people who have first-hand experience, not just course tutors and admissions officers but also current and former students. The second step is to try something out. Whatever your aims in returning to learning - whether recreational, vocational or academic - there are ways of easing yourself in gently. Enrol on a short course in a subject that interests you or take one of the 'return to study' courses which are designed to help you explore your options.

In chapter two, sources of information and advice are discussed in detail. Re-capping briefly, to find out where particular courses are available:

> contact local advice, information and guidance agencies for adults

> consult local and national databases of courses - databases may be available for you to use in the above agencies, or in libraries and Jobcentres

> telephone learndirect - the national helpline for information about courses, on 0800 100 900

> get hold of prospectuses of all local colleges, or colleges in travelling range of home. If considering distance learning, identify possible providers (see chapter five) and get hold of brochures.

Find out as much as you can about each opportunity

Seek to answer the following.
> Where does the course **lead**?
> What does the course **content** cover?
> How is the course **structured and delivered** - does that fit into your lifestyle?
> What about **the course provider** – its reputation, facilities and support services?
> What about the **cost** - put simply, can you afford it?

Let's consider these five questions in more detail.

Where does the course lead?

You may need to consider how useful any certificate or award will be both in terms of openings into careers and jobs and in terms of entry to further professional study or higher education. You need to balance the merits of gaining a general award like an economics

A level, for example, against a specific qualification for a particular trade or occupation.

Some key questions

> - Is the award recognised widely by employers?
> - Is it necessary to achieve a higher position at work or within your profession?
> - Is it a recognised entry qualification for higher-level academic courses?
> - Are you clear about which higher-level courses you could progress onto?
> - Does that qualification help you to achieve your long term goals; for example, is it necessary for the career change you wish to make?

What does the course content cover?

> - You need to get beyond course titles and find out what the course actually covers. For example, even degrees in seemingly straightforward subjects such as history and mathematics vary considerably between institutions. It is important to study something that sustains your interest, so make sure you are aware of the topics covered.
> - Are there decisions about options to be taken that you will need to consider?
> - Are you ready for the demands of the course - or do you need to do some preparatory study first?
> - How is the course assessed? Is that in a manner that suits you?
> - What are the entry requirements, if any? Are you, as an adult applicant, expected to meet them, or can they be relaxed in view of other experience and qualifications that you can offer?

How is the course structured and delivered?

A more practical consideration, but one of equal importance, will concern the way the course is organised and structured. This will have a large bearing on whether it can be successfully combined with your current work and domestic responsibilities.

Chapter 7 - Making your choice

Find a course that suits your personal circumstances

The most common reason for adults to drop out of learning is through being over-committed. When you have conflicting domestic and work responsibilities, study can take a back seat.

Time pressures, more than anything else, can lead to discouragement and disillusionment. Take advantage of the flexibility offered by colleges and other providers to find a course that complements rather than clashes with your other responsibilities. You can always switch to more intensive or full-time courses as you become more confident and committed.

Coping with the additional domestic and social pressures that a return to learning can bring is looked at more fully in the next chapter.

Course structure and delivery - the key questions

➢ How is the course delivered - full-time? part-time? Or through open or distance learning?

➢ How much independent study time is required, outside of the timetabled classroom/learning sessions. How realistic is that for you?

➢ How much flexibility does the course structure offer you? Should you need to take a break from the course, will that present problems? Or is the course structured on a modular or unit basis, which you build up as you go along?

➢ Will you be assigned a personal tutor? What kind and level of support will he/she provide?

Ruth Farrow – full-time student on a Diploma in Higher Education course

> 'Finding myself single with three children at the age of thirty-six, I felt I had reached a cross-roads. I could not earn enough to support my family doing the jobs I had done previously, and I had no qualifications other than a handful of O levels, experience of work in the office, bar, restaurant and retail trade. In order to support my children I needed desperately to improve my chances through education. At first, I looked at the kind of qualifications that would benefit me most financially, but I realised that, if the plan was to

study a subject in a frequently chaotic home, then it would have to be something I wanted passionately to do. I have always had an interest in literature but have never had the time to read the books I'd like or the guidance I felt I needed to find out who the great writers were and why. So I decided to investigate the possibility of doing a degree in English literature with a view to becoming an English teacher in secondary school.

Most of the difficulties I encountered appeared early on. Finding the courage to take on such a challenge and the appropriate course, organising grants and learning how to write essays, all were considerable obstacles. As I progressed I was surprised; I always encountered positive and extremely helpful people who made the whole experience a pleasant adventure. I now find that I am a calmer, more confident person than I ever was. My personal life has improved because of this. My children's attitude towards their own education has improved considerably; being a fellow student and a mother gives a fuller understanding of the teenage world!

My advice to anyone contemplating going back to learning is, do it. No matter how small or large the undertaking, I have always benefited from any form of further education. You are never too old to learn, in fact, once you realise the true importance of a good education it becomes a delight. Though what I do is not easy and quite often feels like an assault course for the mind, there are many books to read in a, sometimes, very noisy house, but the more I learn the more I want to learn. My improvement is slow and steady and my ambitions become wider and wider. Where I once felt in the middle of my life, I now feel at the beginning. There are now many varied possibilities for a future career. Learning for me is a positive force in an often negative and unfair world and I have never regretted my decision to return to learning.'

What about the course provider?

It is wise to find out as much as you can about the course provider, and the facilities and services provided.

> Has the provider a good **reputation**? Do you have contacts who have been on other courses at the same institution – or even better, on the same course as you are considering? Be careful not to put too much weight on one person's opinion, but if you hear certain criticisms repeatedly, you

Chapter 7 - Making your choice

may want to check those aspects out particularly carefully. For example, if people comment on the lack of access to computing facilities, or time it takes to get work marked and returned, you may therefore choose to ask pertinent questions of admissions staff about such aspects, and listen closely to their responses.

- Does the learning provider make adult learners **welcome**?
- What about **learner support**? E.g. extra help with study skills, or support with English and maths?
- Is there an effective **student welfare** service?
- What are the **library** facilities like? Are there sufficient copies of essential texts?
- Are the **IT facilities** sufficient for your needs e.g. wordprocessing or research?
- **Childcare** provision – is it available, are there places available, and where is it sited in relation to your course base?
- **Parking** for students – does it exist, and will space be available when you need it?

These are all aspects of learning that are easy to overlook when considering choice of course or institution, but they could make a crucial difference to the success of your learning. Some of these aspects, including childcare provision and support services, are discussed in more depth in the next chapter.

What about course costs?

Of course, this is the big question! As has been described in the last chapter, this is a complex area. However, assistance or fee remission is available for many students, and, of course, if you are on a government-funded training programme, your training is free. As emphasised in chapter six, don't hesitate to ask about all the 'hidden' costs, such as for books, materials, examination entry fees, or even visits or fieldtrips. And remember to take into account your travelling costs!

Make sure you have a realistic idea of the total cost involved. Don't hesitate to ask about any fee remission or extra assistance, especially if you could not otherwise afford to start the course.

Weighing up the pros and cons

So, you have now identified your options, found out all you possibly can about each, looked into the finances and all the practicalities.

Ideally, you will be left with a shortlist of one course, which meets all your needs! However, life being as it is, it is more likely that you will have narrowed down to a few courses, each of which has various pros and cons, possibly leaving you still uncertain as to the best option.

Firstly, make sure that you have got **all** the information you need. If you still have unanswered questions that prevent you from being able to come to a decision, contact the course provider and ask.

One simple approach to decision making is simply to write down a list of pros and cons for each opportunity. Try to be as specific as you can about each advantage and disadvantage. This process can, in itself, help to crystallise your thoughts. Just seeing the pros and cons written in black and white can help.

Look in particular at the disadvantages you have identified. How great are these? Are they all **really** drawbacks? Perhaps some can be overcome? For example, if costs are one of your drawbacks, are you sure there is no available financial assistance, or ways of paying, that could help? If concerned you may not cope with the written assignments, perhaps there is study skills support that you are not aware of? Always remember there may be 'ways round' perceived problems. Contact the admissions tutor and talk over your concerns with him or her.

Remember, it is always useful to talk over decisions with someone else, preferably someone that is impartial, independent and who has some expertise. Staff based in adult guidance agencies can help you to assess the best learning option for you. Do make use of their services.

Further information

Some or all of the books below should be available in careers centres and adult guidance agencies. As well as those listed, agencies may have databases of occupations and learning opportunities that you can consult, or computerised career guidance systems, such as Adult Directions, that generates job suggestions based on the user's likes and dislikes. Adult guidance agencies may also hold Keynotes, a series of careers guidance leaflets for adults.

Chapter 7 - Making your choice

Build Your Own Rainbow – a workbook for career and life management, published by Lifeskills International, £15.00.

Occupations – an annually published reference book containing information on jobs. Includes information about entry requirements, training and late entry. Published by COIC.

The Penguin Careers Guide – provides information about careers, including information about qualification requirements, part-time work and job sharing opportunities for each occupation.

Coming Back to Learning

CHAPTER 8
Taking the plunge

> 'I'm very happy with the progress I've made and I know that I wouldn't have got here if I hadn't taken the plunge all those years ago. So come on in, the water's lovely!'

The words of one happy returner!

The previous chapters of this book have taken you through the different ways you can learn and the qualifications you can gain. Hopefully, it has answered a few questions and problems over finance. If you've made some choices, based on this information, it's time to consider taking the plunge.

Perhaps the biggest barrier preventing more adults from studying is psychological. Returning to learning represents a step into the unknown. It generates concerns about doing coursework, writing essays and taking exams. If you have been away from full-time education for some years, it is easy to question your own abilities or to fear failure. And there is some understandable unease about placing yourself in new situations and environments.

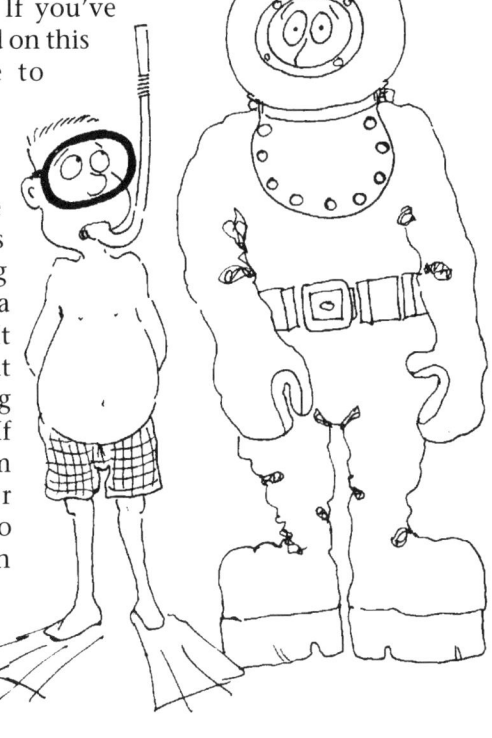

Preparing for your return

These concerns can be summarised in a single question: will I be able to cope? The answer, as the individual stories throughout this book illustrate, is that, with good planning and guidance at the outset, most people manage extremely successfully. The main thing is to make sure that you are likely to enjoy your studies. You may need to keep your motivation up for several years, and pressures you may face during the course are not always apparent at the outset.

Sandra Small – into teaching via a PGCE course

> 'For many years I had been interested in primary teaching, but always dismissed it as impossible; after all, raising three children didn't exactly leave a great deal of time to indulge in pursuing my own career! As a result, the idea remained firmly on the back burner and remained just that – an idea. For many years I contented myself with helping out at my son's primary school as a classroom assistant and serving as a governor, all of which turned out to be invaluable experience. As soon as I felt the time was right for my family, I applied for training. To my surprise, I was called for an interview to the University of the West of England, in Bristol. The interview was very relaxed and informal, and I found that my 'work experience' stood me in good stead. I was offered a place on the PGCE course, starting September '99 .

> The first day at Bristol was nerve racking, and I felt very old, but I quickly realised that I wasn't the only one who was nervous. There was an interesting mix of ages and life experiences; for example, a fellow student began the course having recently had her second child, whereas others has returned from a year out after taking their first degree. We were allocated to a tutor group of about 20 students and worked mainly within that group. The group began to 'gel' surprisingly quickly, perhaps due to the intensity of the course; we supported and learned from each other. The course was completely different to a degree course, being vocational – we were told at the outset to expect a 9 to 5 day at least, with very little free time as there was so much to cram into one year. The run-up to Christmas was particularly hectic for those of us with family responsibilities; we definitely felt the extra pressure! I found the travelling exhausting, and the volume of work soul-destroying at times – I still remember forcing myself to stay awake on the

Chapter 8 - Taking the plunge

train to finish some prescribed reading! However, the feeling of achievement on completing the course was unforgettable, like winning a gold medal! Looking back, I think the support and understanding of my family was crucial; the whole venture would have been impossible without that – unless you happen to be Wonder Woman!

To any would-be mature students out there, I would recommend the following points as a means of staying sane:

- *If you have family responsibilities, make sure everyone is supportive and realises the need to help out – outline <u>how</u> they can help if you need to!*
- *Be organised and prioritise – you can't do it all at once! Set yourself realistic, achievable targets.*
- *Allocate a bit of time each week just for you so that you can relax and escape for a while – go to the gym, see a film or just soak in the bath! It's amazing how it recharges the batteries, and you produce better work as a result.*
- *Don't be afraid to ask for help if you need to – it keeps problems in perspective.*
- *Lastly, <u>enjoy</u> being a student – good luck!'*

As Sandra says, coming back to learning can be challenging. This chapter looks at some of the problems adults face and the ways that these can be tackled. It is organised into two parts:

- study skills
- domestic and social pressures.

The first half, on study skills, covers essay and examination phobia, describes ways of preparing for study and looks at the support available to those at university and college. The second half of this chapter deals with some of the domestic and social pressures of returning to learning. It examines how to make the time to study, and tackles issues such as how to combine learning with looking after children and dependants.

The message is that you do not have to manage everything on your own. There is support available to help you overcome problems. Increasingly, colleges are putting extra emphasis on 'learner support services', which are designed both to help students learn more effectively and to care for their welfare.

Study skills

Mature students sometimes have a reflex inferiority complex. They feel that their work is not up to standard, that they will not be able to write essays, and that they will flunk exams. If your previous experience of education at school was not very positive, or if you were not very successful, then these fears can seem more like home truths than mere conjectures. The facts, however, speak otherwise. Studies of the performance of students at university show that:

> - good A level results are no guarantee of success; in fact, there is little correlation between entry qualifications and final degree performance
> - older students tend to do better than those that join university straight from school or sixth-form college
> - those that enter university without traditional qualifications do as well as those admitted with the standard two or three A levels.

There have been few similar studies in further education, but the anecdotal evidence from talking to course tutors and lecturers all points in the same direction: mature students do well. Older students are generally welcome in further and higher education because they work harder, are well motivated and, with their valuable experience, they contribute more to courses.

It should be reassuring to know that adults returning to education tend to do well. But how do you know whether you will cope? How can you improve your study skills? There are several practical steps you can take by:

> - confronting essay and exam phobia
> - preparing for study
> - using learner support services
> - building confidence.

Essay and exam phobia

Education conjures up visions of essays and examinations. When they leave school or college for the last time, many people experience

Chapter 8 - Taking the plunge

huge relief from knowing that it is finally over. The thought of going through it all again can be a major barrier to returning to education. So, how do you overcome the fear of essays and exams?

The most important thing to do is to put the problem into perspective. Essays can seem difficult but often the difficulties are not due to lack of ability. One of the most common problems arises from the fact that adults set themselves high standards; they want to do well and judge themselves harshly. They fear failure and 'loss of face'. Consequently, if you think that everything you write is not good enough, it becomes very difficult to write anything.

Again, exams can seem daunting because they are perceived to be the sole or major determinant of the final result. In recent years, however, there have been many changes in the way that courses are assessed. There has been a move away from complete reliance on traditional examinations. Both in further and higher education, there is more use of continuous assessment and assignment-based assessment. In vocational education, the trend is towards competence-based courses; you are judged on your performance in real situations, rather than your ability to pass theoretical exams.

Like any phobia, the way to deal with worries about essays or exams is to confront them head-on. The key is practice: the more you do, the easier it becomes. If you are out of practice – unlike school-leavers, most adults will have taken a lengthy break from education – there are some practical steps you can take. There are two main options which are considered in more detail below. First, you can undertake some preparatory study, before starting a longer course, which will help you build up confidence and develop study skills. Second, you can take advantage of the support offered by many colleges and universities through learning resource centres and similar facilities.

Study preparation

There are many courses which are specifically designed to help adults prepare for a return to study. Courses with titles such as 'return to study' or 'second chance to learn' prepare you for longer programmes in further and higher education. Access courses are designed for adults who wish to take degrees and other higher education qualifications but lack the formal entry requirements.

All these courses include a specific element devoted to helping you learn effectively. Typically, this will include practical advice on:

- study skills
- use of learning resources
- examination techniques.

But, importantly, these programmes also offer a more gradual return to education. They are an opportunity to test the water, to assess your options and, crucially, to build some confidence in your own abilities. So, if you are lacking confidence, an Access course may be beneficial even if you have the qualifications to be accepted immediately onto a degree course.

An alternative way of preparing for study is to take a distance learning course. For example, the National Extension College runs courses on study skills with titles such as 'How to write essays', 'How to succeed in exams and assessments', 'How to manage your study time' and 'How to study effectively'.

The Open University has several useful study packs. These include short taster courses designed to get people back into the swing of studying before starting a longer course. The Openings programme of short introductory courses gives you the chance to:

- work on your study skills
- build up your confidence
- get a taste of your chosen subject
- decide what you want to study in the future.

All new OU students are sent a preparatory package before the start of a course to help them brush up their skills.

Finally, there is the do-it-yourself approach. You can prepare for a course by background reading, using self-study materials and even by doing practice essays. If you have been accepted onto a course, then ask tutors what would be the most useful preparation to undertake to help bring you up to speed.

Learner support services

Learner support services is a catch-all term for the measures that many colleges and universities are introducing to help their students learn effectively. These services are increasingly common, not least because of demand created by the numbers of people returning to education after several years away from studying. But the measures are also designed to support new ways of teaching, which place less

Chapter 8 - Taking the plunge

emphasis on lectures and seminars and provide more opportunities for supported private study and group work with other students.

Help with study skills comes in several guises. The skills covered will typically include note-taking, writing, revision methods and exam techniques. In some courses, it is an integral part of the learning programme. Some colleges and universities have set up study skills centres or provide other resources which students can use on an occasional basis when they have a specific problem. Others rely on advice through more informal contacts with personal tutors.

Many colleges pay particular attention to those with disabilities or with specific learning difficulties. This includes help for those who have visual or hearing impairments and those who have conditions such as dyslexia that can affect studying. In addition, they provide tutors to help people improve basic numeracy and literacy and offer a range of English language teaching for speakers of other languages.

The message is that if you do find coping with the coursework or exams difficult (and everybody has problems at some stage), then there are sources of help and advice; you can approach tutors, fellow students or staff in learning resources centres. You do not **have** to work through every problem by yourself.

Confidence

Many older students expect to be 'found out', expect to be found wanting. It rarely happens. Few mature students drop out simply because they cannot cope with the academic work, although many have doubts at the start – the younger students are brighter, the college made a mistake in admitting me, my coursework isn't up to standard.

The main point to emphasise is that this passes. Worries are usually more to do with confidence and self-belief than academic ability. You gain confidence from completing the first course assignments successfully. You gain confidence from your fellow students, who are often extremely helpful, you make new friends and you find out that they are certainly not the masterminds you might have assumed them to be.

Tutors and lecturers are generally supportive. They do not tend to patronise or talk down to adults; as mentioned above, many actively welcome the contribution and enthusiasm that older people bring to the classroom. But equally, they are aware that adults have uncertainties about returning to education, so they try to offer encouragement and to help people build up self-confidence.

Nonetheless, in the final analysis, it is up to you. And most people surprise themselves with what they can do. You may start with anxieties and doubts, but you will end with a sense of achievement.

> *'Don't take on anything you feel you're going to struggle with, set yourself goals, be positive and you will enjoy the experience'.*

Domestic and social pressures

Education offers the possibility of change. For many mature students it provides a big stimulus and lift, but for their partners it may be threatening or stressful. They can feel that they are being left behind or missing out. It is perhaps understandable that relationships can suffer; indeed, some fail. But there are other, perhaps more mundane, pressures that arise from the effort of trying to juggle too many balls at once through running a home and earning a living, in addition to studying.

As a result, though mature students rarely drop out of courses because of lack of ability or lack of money, some find that it becomes difficult to cope with the worry of how their studying affects family and partners.

Studying need not be stressful or pressurised, but you need to be able to face up to the demands it generates. Before the course, you should be aware of some of the potential problems and pitfalls.

Key questions to ask

- Can you find the time each week needed to attend classes, to study and complete assignments?
- Will you be able to combine studying with caring for children and dependant relatives?
- Will partners feel excluded or neglected?
- Do you need to spend nights or weeks away from home?
- Is travel to and from college convenient or manageable?

It may not be possible to answer all these questions satisfactorily before you start out. Some problems will only materialise during the course. But there are ways of anticipating problems and establishing support systems. You can make things easier for yourself by enlisting the help of friends and relatives. You can also benefit from the increasing amount of support available from colleges and

Chapter 8 - Taking the plunge

universities. Some provide practical help with childcare, a few offer support with transport and most run some kind of welfare service.

Support systems

Perhaps the most obvious way of minimising the pressures is to plan education wisely. Be aware of the time, money and effort required, and be careful not to take on too much. This is not written to put you off studying, rather to suggest that you need to find the right course at the right time. And you need the support systems to help you manage.

What this means in practice will very much depend on your own personal circumstances. For example, if you are bringing up children then there are a number of issues to weigh up in deciding when to return to learning. When children are pre-school age, studying is difficult unless there is affordable nursery provision. Even when children are at school, full-time education might be impractical unless you can arrange after-school and holiday care. You need to think about finding the time to study; with young children you have the evenings free, as they grow older you might need to negotiate free time with your partner.

If you are working, you need to weigh the effect on your career of any study breaks. You might want to avoid taking on an extra activity during periods when your job is particularly demanding. You need to balance the effects of any possible loss of income against future benefits.

Whatever decision you make, you are more likely to make a success of education if you receive support from others. This can come from several sources.

Family

If you are married or in a long-term relationship, it is important to have the backing of your partner. You need moral support, rather than having your efforts belittled. You may need practical support such as an agreement to look after the kids at the weekend so that you have peace and quiet to study.

Friends

In returning to learning, you may sometimes feel that you have to prove something, not just to yourself but to sceptical friends and colleagues. Ideally, friends should be on your side and a source of encouragement, but if they are disparaging, use it as a source of strength and resolve to prove them wrong.

Fellow students

Education can be isolating if you are studying at home alone, and just attending college for classes. Find time to socialise with fellow students, if for no other reason than to reassure yourself that other people are having to deal with the same kinds of problems as you. Some universities have mature students' societies that organise social activities and act as an informal support system for older students.

Employer

If you are working, your employer may be prepared to help you organise your time better so that there is room for study. Some employers will grant flexible hours or a temporary switch to part-time working, others allow (unpaid) sabbaticals and study leave.

Childcare

Education providers recognise that many adults, especially women, are effectively prevented from returning to education unless they can find adequate nursery and crèche facilities for their children while they attend classes. Many courses aimed at women, such as programmes for those wishing to return to work or daytime adult education classes, simply would not attract sufficient numbers to be viable unless free or cheap childcare were made available.

Chapter 8 - Taking the plunge

University and college nurseries

An increasing number of universities and colleges have nurseries to look after the children of both staff and students. Places are often extremely limited, so you should apply as soon as possible. Contact the Student Services office of your chosen HE institution to find out what's available and how much it will cost. Policy on nursery fees varies enormously; some colleges heavily subsidise the service, others set fees to recoup their costs.

Even if they have very few facilities themselves, colleges and universities may be able to provide useful information on local childcare facilities. As one returner remarks:

> *'Even the college support network is geared towards helping the mature students; they even helped me arrange a childminder for when I'm attending lessons'.*

Looking after school-age children

Colleges are slowly waking up to the fact that parental responsibilities do not end when children start attending school. Some have introduced more flexibility into the timetable, making it easier for parents to take classes in the middle of the day, and so leaving them the time to take and fetch children to and from school. Some run programmes that coincide with school terms, taking breaks during holidays and half-term.

However, many courses still overlap with school holidays or have classes scheduled outside school hours. Although some colleges and universities now run schemes for school-age children, in practice most parents will have to make their own arrangements for their children after school and during holidays.

Other sources of help

If you have to make your own arrangements for your children while you are attending classes, then your options include helpful friends and relatives, childminders, state nurseries, private nurseries and play centres, and after-school play schemes.

The Government's National Childcare Strategy is designed to help overcome the problems of childcare while you are learning. At present, there are free nursery places five mornings per week for all four-year-olds: some in private and state nurseries but, increasingly, primary schools are creating their own nursery units to accommodate them. By 2001/2002 the expectation is that there will be free nursery places for 66% of all three-year-olds.

To get a fuller picture of your options, you should explore all avenues of financial support and practical advice.

learndirect helpline (0800 100 900) can advise on childcare provision for people returning to learning.

Gingerbread is a network of self-help support groups for single parents. Local groups may be contacted through the national office (Tel: 020 7336 8183).

Childcare Link 08000 9602 96 – a national freephone helpline to direct parents in the search for local childcare. 9am to 9pm Monday – Friday; 9am to midday on Saturday. www.childcarelink.gov.uk

Daycare Trust – Shoreditch Town Hall Annexe, 380 Old Street, London EC1V 9LT. Tel: 020 7739 2866. Can advise parents and employers on the quality and accessibility of childcare. www.daycaretrust.org.uk

Transport

The provision, time and cost of travel can cause persistent hassle to those returning to learning. Long and frequent journeys backwards and forwards to college don't just cost money; they eat up time and they can be tiring, adding significantly to stress levels.

There are only a limited number of ways in which you can restrict travel demands. The most obvious is to attend a college or education provider that is conveniently located. Unfortunately this may not be practicable: local colleges may not be very accessible, or they may not run the courses you wish to take. If you have a difficult journey, you could try to organise a lift arrangement with fellow students. Ask if classes, tutorials and workshops can be arranged to minimise the number of journeys you have to make each week.

In general, education providers do realise that travel difficulties can restrict access to studying. Within their financial constraints, some try to offer support with transport.

Welfare services

Under the broad banner of student services, colleges and universities provide a range of practical help for students who have problems or are troubled in some way. This has two main strands, one concerned with effective learning (see learner support services above), the other with health, finance and welfare problems.

Although older students are often the last to admit that they have problems (after all, one of the more dubious benefits of maturity is that you are supposedly more able to work through problems and fend for yourself), it is useful to know that such help exists. If you do have a problem that is affecting your coursework, or if your course is having an adverse effect on the rest of your life, then there are people who can provide advice and support.

The specific services vary from institution to institution. However, most provide some of the following:

- confidential personal counselling
- advice on welfare rights and welfare benefits
- information on matters of finance
- educational guidance and careers advice
- assistance with childcare
- health care and/or health education.

Colleges organise this welfare service in various ways and under a number of names, including a student advisory and counselling service, or a counselling and support service. Some institutions link counselling services with educational and careers guidance, others with financial and grants advice.

You should note that welfare services can sometimes be very stretched. This means that you may have to wait some time for an appointment with a counsellor. However, most services dispense general information and advice to anyone who drops by. Note that students' unions are another source of help; many have a welfare office.

Applying for a course

If, having noted all the points raised in this chapter, you are ready to 'take the plunge', you need to apply for the course of your choice.

For places on most educational courses at colleges of further education, or those offered by independent providers

You should apply directly to the course provider. Recruitment for further education courses run at FE colleges is done directly by the colleges themselves.

Most colleges have streamlined application procedures through admissions and guidance units. The main enrolment period for courses is usually at the beginning of September. However, many colleges start postal or telephone enrolments in May or June, so courses can fill early. Some courses and flexible learning programmes recruit throughout the year and, in general, it is possible to join courses after the start of term providing they are not full. Admissions staff should be able to advise you about courses, flexible learning options, course costs and student facilities such as childcare.

Most applications to higher education courses (degrees and HNDs) run at FE colleges are now done via UCAS.

For full-time courses at degree and diploma of higher education level

Courses at universities and colleges fall into two categories.

Those for which you apply direct to the university or college running the course

If you wish to study on any part-time or short course, a distance learning course or on most postgraduate courses, you apply direct to the university or college. (Exceptions to this are postgraduate teacher-training courses and social work.)

Those for which you apply through a central admissions service

To study on a full-time (or sandwich) first degree, diploma or Higher National Diploma (HND) course, or for postgraduate qualifications in teacher training or social work, you apply through a **central admissions service**. This processes applications to all institutions offering HE courses in the UK. Sometimes referred to as clearing houses, details of the separate admissions services are given below. Each service deals with a specific range of courses.

Chapter 8 - Taking the plunge

You can apply at any time, although you will stand more chance of acceptance if you make an early application. For full-time degree courses, for example, applicants are advised to apply between September and December in the year prior to entry. However, many universities are sympathetic to late applications from mature students.

In general, universities are happy to advise potential mature students on applications procedures. Before making an application through the central admissions system, it might be worth while talking to staff at the institution at which you wish to study. If you are in any doubt about where and how to apply for a particular course, then speak to the admissions office of the university running that course.

The central admissions services are:

Universities and Colleges Admissions Service (UCAS). UCAS handles applications for almost all full-time and sandwich courses at universities and higher education colleges leading to the award of a degree, diploma of higher education (DipHE) and higher national diploma (HND). Applications forms, acknowledgement cards and UCAS Handbook available from: UCAS, PO Box 67, Cheltenham GL52 3ZD.

UCAS now operates an electronic application system which, in the future, will become the accepted way of making applications. Website: www.ucas.ac.uk

Graduate Teacher Training Registry (GTTR). GTTR is the clearing house for postgraduate certificate in education (PGCE) courses. Application forms are available from: GTTR, Rosehill, New Barn Lane, Cheltenham GL52 3LZ. Website: www.gttr.ac.uk

Social Work Admissions System (SWAS). SWAS should be used for most Diploma in Social Work courses. A few courses, mainly part-time, require direct application to colleges. Check prospectuses. Applicants are dealt with on a first-come, first-served basis. Application forms available from: SWAS, Rosehill, New Barn Lane, Cheltenham GL52 3LZ.

Nurses and Midwives Admissions System (NMAS). For nursing and midwifery diploma courses. Apply to NMAS, Rosehill, New Barn Lane, Cheltenham GL52 3LZ. Website: www.nmas.ac.uk

It is always worth making a direct approach to a university initially, particularly if you are only able to study at your local institution. Many admissions officers are sympathetic to prospective mature students and will provide general information and advice. Provide them with a detailed CV, and see if you can arrange an appointment.

As a general rule, the earlier you apply for educational courses, the better your chances of acceptance. This is certainly true for very popular courses like the Open University's arts programmes. Do not wait for the 'right time' to make an application. Apply when the mood strikes. You might find that you are pushing at an open door: there may be late cancellations or some places may be held for 'non-traditional' entrants.

For a Government-funded training place

For Work-based Learning for Adults (Training for Work in Scotland) – the training programme for unemployed adults from 25 to 63 – your starting point will normally be at the Jobcentre. Your eligibility will need to be checked, and other necessary administration undertaken.

Further information

Exam Survival – published by Trotman, £8.99.

Learning in Later Life – published by Kogan Page, £19.99. Published September 2000.

The Good Study Guide – by Andrew Northedge, published by the Open University, £8.99 is helpful in developing study skills for OU foundation courses.

How to Study – published by Kogan Page, £8.99.

Second Chances – is a DfEE publication which may be available for reference in careers libraries. It can also be found on the DfEE website. www.dfee.gov.uk/secondchances

Keynotes – a series of careers guidance leaflets for adults, published by Lifetime Careers Publishing. The series may be available for reference in careers libraries.

To find details of all the further and higher education courses on offer, turn to chapter five for a list of course directories. These should be available for consultation in libraries and careers centres.

CHAPTER 9
Building on your learning

The vast majority of older graduates felt that their time in higher education had been one of the highlights of their lives – according to an Association of Graduate Careers Advisory Services survey.

Returning to learning can be an extremely positive experience. All the profiles contributed to this book endorse the fact that learning something new can provide a welcome mental challenge, giving people something to aim for, while, at the same time, developing new interests. And, often, at the end of a course of study there can be a sense of anticlimax; almost inevitably, people ask themselves 'What next?'

Considerations

This chapter suggests some ways of continuing with – and building on – your learning. It looks briefly at how you can weigh up and explore options in academic learning, vocational education and in employment. But, before that, it is worth underlining three points:

➢ You do **not** have to follow a plan. Not everything we do has to be for a particular goal or purpose. Studying is

- satisfying in its own right, and you can choose to do it for fun and general interest, when you have the time, the inclination and the opportunity.
- If, however, you do have a precise aim in mind, such as achieving qualifications essential for entry to a career, or for career advancement, then it is worth doing careful planning at the outset, and interim checks, to make sure your plan remains valid and on track.
- Ideas change and develop over time. At every stage of your learning pathway, consult with people who can advise you on taking your next step. Sources of help and advice are listed at the end of chapters seven and nine.

'How much my re-education has helped my career opportunities, only time will tell. What is apparent is that it hasn't done them any harm – and, who knows, maybe life does begin at forty after all!'

Many people – training providers, human resources managers, careers advisers, course tutors and directors of studies – can help you plan your next move. Keen to promote lifelong learning, all education suppliers embrace the concept of progression in studies, and can offer people clear information on further courses, routes towards higher qualifications and vocational accreditation that can help you find employment. Many people will not achieve their aims through a single course. Instead, there will be a longer (some would say lifelong) process of personal and career development.

Onwards and upwards

Adults often return to learning with some trepidation, unsure about their abilities. Typically, once they start, their confidence increases and they develop a taste for study.

'The more I learn, the more I want to learn!'

So, for many people, a natural next step is to take another course, motivated either by a desire to push themselves further and explore new interests, or to gain higher and more useful qualifications. It is now much easier to progress from one course to another. One reason is that the majority of further and higher education programmes have flexible entry requirements for adult applicants. In some cases, completion of any previous course is taken as sufficient evidence of your ability to study. The widespread introduction of credit

Chapter 9 - Building on your learning

transfer schemes makes it possible to use accreditation from your current course to gain acceptance onto further programmes. Also, depending on the course of study you have been following, it may be possible to gain exemption from parts of a new course (see the section on accreditation of prior learning or APL in chapter four).

Jacki Ciereszko – encouraged by success

> 'I first started back at college three years ago, after I was made redundant, and took a database and a spreadsheet course.
>
> Once I had found another job, I had to do a DTP course so that I could actually **do** my new job! Then, I had an 18-month break from college, but soon found the pull to go back too strong! I like to keep my IT skills as up-to-date as possible, with exam results to prove that I can do it.
>
> The next course I completed – paid for by my employer – was in web design, so then I was able to design and set up a multi-page website with confidence, as well as complete a site started by someone else. In my personal life, I am now able to offer my web design services to others – for instance, my riding club.
>
> I didn't find any problems when I was doing my courses, but now I want to progress and there doesn't seem to be any further courses that fulfil my current learning need to advance in multimedia design.
>
> The positive benefits have been that I now feel confident enough to try the Information Business Technology Level 3 course and retake an exam I failed three years ago. Also, I am looking into which course to try next term. Maybe pottery! I am going to carry on learning as I feel you should keep your mind active. I would like to do the pilot Internet Technologies course my local college is running.
>
> If you are considering going back to college, DO IT, you've got nothing to lose; the tutors and instructors are all there to help you achieve your aims/goals. Find out if you are entitled to any financial help and, if not, do it in easy stages. But, most of all, enjoy it! Learning can be and is fun.'

Colleges and adult education centres have advisers who can help you plan a further programme of study. Sometimes, this planning element is an integral part of the course. For example, adult returner courses are explicitly designed to help you assess your future options, and most people naturally progress from these programmes to other courses, with the same, or another, training or education supplier.

It is important to emphasise that there are no set pathways in the learning process. You will soon find that learning can lead in many directions, each with different outcomes. Even if your learning has been purely vocational you can make excellent use of the skills and attributes you have acquired in quite different settings.

Watersheds

There are several important points in the learning process where you need to make careful choices about your options. Of course, this does not apply to adult leisure and recreational studies, where the only significant decision is whether to take courses that lead to a recognised award or whether to continue with study for its own sake. These are not mutually incompatible, but adult education centres tend to draw a sharp distinction between courses which are assessed and those which are free from testing.

For most people, there is a need to weigh up the benefits and drawbacks of progressing to higher education, or for those that have achieved a first degree, the possibility and desirability of taking your studies to postgraduate level.

Key questions

If you are considering further study at the end of your present course, perhaps the best advice is to apply these five tests:

- ➢ Have I got the time?
- ➢ Can I afford it?
- ➢ Will I enjoy it?
- ➢ Would further study knit with or build on my previous qualifications?
- ➢ Will it improve my job prospects or benefit my career?

Chapter 9 - Building on your learning

On to higher education?

Following advanced education – that is, courses which lead to qualifications at level 3, i.e. of a standard equivalent to A levels, a double award Vocational A level or a BTEC National Diploma – the key decision is whether to progress to higher educational studies. Surveys of people who have attained level 3 qualifications show that around a third of this group leave full-time education and go straight into employment, while almost two thirds decide to progress to higher education – the majority studying for degrees, others taking a BTEC Higher National Diploma (HND) and, a few, a Diploma in Higher Education (DipHE). Of course, those who decide to find paid employment at this stage can continue to make progress in their learning through work-based training and off-the-job study.

Higher and higher?

For graduates, the choice is between:

> employment
> postgraduate education
> training.

Destination figures for 1999 graduates show that 18.6% continued with further study or training, while 69.2% found work in the UK or abroad. Continuing with full-time education or training can be a useful alternative if attractive jobs seem scarce, or, for entry to some professions, such as teaching, where a postgraduate qualification is essential. However, you need to be very wary of continuing studying simply because you have found nothing better to do. After all, there is no guarantee that the job market will be any different when you finish postgraduate education. Department for Education and Employment research found that while a professional qualification or Masters degree can increase your earning potential, a postgraduate diploma or a doctorate has no significant impact on earnings. In an AGCAS survey, 20% of all mature graduates (recorded as those aged 25 or over on course completion) chose to continue with further study or training after graduation. This proportion tends to increase with age.

Off to work

For many people, the long-term aim of returning to study or training is to be able to put what you have learned to some use. This does not have to be through **paid employment**; there are alternatives. Certainly, in today's labour market, more people are **self-employed** or work on a freelance basis. In Spring 1999, over three million people were working for themselves in Britain – a little less than 12% of the active labour force. Some use their new learning as a springboard to set up their own businesses. Quite a number of people who don't need to increase their income, or who have some flexibility in terms of demands on their time, are able to step off the employment conveyor belt and take up **voluntary work**. If you can't find a suitable job at present, time spent on worthwhile projects can be a valuable way of demonstrating to future employers your determination and ability to work. In some fields, it can be the only way of getting the experience necessary to enter paid employment or to being accepted onto a training course. You should note that organisations like VSO (Voluntary Service Overseas), which have been traditionally associated with young people, increasingly seek mature, even retired people with greater experience and a comprehensive range of skills. Only, be wary of considering voluntary work as a soft option: the scope varies enormously and may require a special sort of personal commitment.

No job guarantee!

If, however, your goal is to find work after a course, or to get a better job, then there are several factors to take into account. Perhaps the most important point to stress is that although learning can be a useful stepping stone to full employment, it does not offer any guarantees. Secondly, your choice of course can clearly be a determining factor. For example, the majority of newly-qualified business studies graduates find jobs within six months of gaining awards. Graduates in medicine and dentistry can effectively walk into jobs. But, even with a degree in information technology – despite its obvious vocational relevance – six months after graduation, unemployment is running at around 6%, just slightly over the average rate of unemployment for all graduates – 5.7%.

However, many graduate employers are not so much interested in the subject of an applicant's degree, as by their potential to succeed in the job. In this context, mature graduates, who present

Chapter 9 - Building on your learning

their accumulated skills, qualifications and experience to advantage, may be a step ahead in the employability stakes. In fact, *What Do Graduates Do?* – an annual publication of the Association of Graduate Careers Advisory Services (AGCAS) – reports that 63% of all mature graduates in 1999 had obtained full employment within six months of graduation.

What do employers want?

Perhaps the key to moving successfully from education into employment can be expressed by the phrase – ' realism, but not defeatism'. Although it may take time, it is important to research the present and future state of the industry you want to enter, to have studied movement in the related job market, and to understand the specific skills that recruiting employers seek. Certainly, recent experience of work in the occupational area, gained either:

- from a placement undertaken during your course
- through vacation or part-time work while you have been studying
- by working in a voluntary capacity

can be a considerable advantage, as mature learners can demonstrate that they have both commercial understanding and a grasp of modern ways of working in business or industry.

Some people limit their own prospects by concentrating too much on their qualifications rather than on the more general skills that they have acquired. In fact, many employers look for generic, rather than specific, skills. This is particularly true in graduate recruitment, where many employers look at the whole person and not so much at the subject or class of their degree. So, recognise and emphasise your 'transferable' skills. These are the key skills, graduate skills, personal qualities and other attributes that can be applied across a variety of work situations, and can include an ability to:

- manage and interpret information
- work in pressurised and stressful situations
- communicate clearly and accurately
- work well both alone and in teams
- get on well with other people, including customers, clients and fellow staff
- act ethically.

Try to avoid being defensive about your maturity, which can be an advantage rather than a disadvantage. In some occupational areas, employers will be looking specifically for people with experience of the world of work and maturity; areas like social work, adult education, personnel work, health and community work, guidance and counselling. Whatever you do, it will be worth highlighting previous successful work experience, even if it is in areas unrelated to those for which you are applying.

Ageism

Perhaps, for many adults, the crucial issue concerns employers' attitudes to the recruitment of older workers and staff. The labour market can be tough on older people and, yet, the prediction is that by the year 2010, almost 40% of the labour force will be aged 45 or older. This age group makes up 35% of all workers in 2000. The Government is fighting to combat ageism in the workplace through a recent initiative – the voluntary *Code of Practice on Age Diversity in Employment* – which suggests that employers should think twice before applying age limits to their recruitment and selection procedures, and, instead, assess applicants purely on the suitability of their qualifications, skills and experience. In practice, some industries and professions continue to show a more flexible attitude than others. For example, it is estimated that some 60% of older graduates still enter the public sector where employment practices, on the whole, are less discriminatory.

Many companies, who were happy to shed older employees a few years back, have come to agree with the propositions that older workers are more reliable than the young, they bring useful experience to an organisation, and that they are often very keen productive employees with a good attitude to work and 'a lot of mileage left in them'.

Careers advisers paint a similar picture. The Association of Graduate Careers Advisory Services (AGCAS) stresses that mature students have many positive attributes that are valued by employers; they mention previous work experience, commitment, determination, stability and adaptability to new situations. Against that, mature students can come across badly at interviews, appearing to be low in confidence, sometimes inflexible, and poorly informed about the demands of the occupation and the needs of the employer within a particular industrial sector.

Chapter 9 - Building on your learning

Do recognise that you can get help and advice. There are courses, informal support groups, books and self-study packs that cover the spectrum from preparing job applications and writing CVs to practising interview techniques. And, there are numerous resources which can provide advice on your best options and through which you can get detailed information about current job opportunities.

The last word

'My improvement is slow and steady and my ambitions become wider and wider. Where I once felt in the middle of my life, I now feel at the beginning. There are now many varied possibilities for a future career. Learning for me is a positive force in an often negative and unfair world and I have never regretted my decision to return to learning.'

Further information

At this point, the book comes full circle because the organisations and agencies that can help you make initial decisions on an education programme to suit you can also advise on next steps. All the organisations mentioned in chapter two are able to provide guidance on selecting further educational options. Many of these organisations will hold careers information, and may also offer help with a return to work.

In addition, learning suppliers offer a variety of practical help to their students. Some of this help may be quite informal; for example, all tutors can advise on progression routes in their own educational sphere. But, all colleges are able to provide professional careers advice and counselling, either through their own careers guidance service or through links with the local careers service provider. Every UK university operates a careers service for their own students, staffed by specialists in graduate careers. All careers centres hold a full range of information and occupational resources.

If you are unemployed, the local Jobcentre run by the Employment Service is a first port of call. Their telephone helpline Employment Direct: 0845 60 60 234, can help you in your search for work. Whatever your setting, you can be put in touch with recruiting employers or given access to a database of European vacancies – together with the help of a European adviser. The Employment Service also has its own website through which you can access job vacancies: www.employmentservice.gov.uk/

All careers organisations hold useful publications on jobseeking, and may provide internet access to reach websites specifically for jobseekers. In searching for work, study the national and local press, specific journals that are the mouthpieces of particular industries, and the range of weekly appointments magazines that carry national and regional vacancies. These publications are normally held in your local public reference library.

Three resources are highlighted from a very wide field:

AGCAS graduate occupational information booklets written by careers advisers and information officers in universities. This wide range of booklets is being continually revised, and some titles are of special interest to mature students. AGCAS booklets are frequently held in careers services libraries. You can also access graduate labour market information on their website: www.prospects.csu.ac.uk

CRAC/Hobsons *Casebook 2001* series: These give an overview of particular industries or occupations, with detail about the opportunities available, together with case studies of recent graduates. In addition to specific industrial sector *Casebooks*, recent titles include *Equal Opportunities ... for Career Women 2001; ...for Disabled Graduates 2001; ... for Ethnic Minorities 2001*. Further information on the *Casebooks* is available from:

Net That Job – by Irene Krechowiecka, published by Kogan Page, price £8.99.

Publishers' addresses

This list gives details of publishers referred to in the book, other than those where contact details are provided within the text.

Butterworth Heinemann – Lineacre House, Jordan Hill, Oxford OX2 8DP. Tel: 01865 310366.

Cassell and Co – Stanley House, 3 Fleet's Lane, Poole BH15 3AJ. Tel: 01202 665432.

COIC – PO Box 298a, Thames Ditton, Surrey KT7 0ZS. Tel: 020 8957 5030.

Hobsons Publishing plc – 159-173 St John Street, London EC1V 4DR. Tel: 020 7336 6633. For CRAC publications.

How To Books Ltd – Plymbridge Distributors Ltd, Estover Road, Plymouth PL6 7PZ. Tel: 01752 202301.

ISCO – 12A Princess Way, Camberley, Surrey GU15 3SP. Tel: 01276 21188.

Kogan Page – 120 Pentonville Road, London N1 9JN. Tel: 020 7278 0433.

Lifeskills International – Wharfbank House, Ilkley Road, Otley LS21 3JP. Tel: 01943 851144.

Lifetime Careers Publishing – 7 Ascot Court, White Horse Business Park, Trowbridge BA14 0XA. Tel: 01225 716023.

NIACE – 21 De Montfort Street, Leicester LE1 7GE. Tel: 0116 204 4269.

Penguin Books – Bath Road, Harmondsworth, West Drayton, Middlesex UB7 0DA. Tel: 020 8757 4000.

Trotman & Co – 2 The Green, Richmond, Surrey TW9 1PL. Tel: 0870 900 2665.

UCAS - Rosehill, New Barn Lane, Cheltenham GL52 3LZ. Tel: 01242 222444.

Vacation Work Publications – 9 Park End Street, Oxford OX1 1HJ. Tel: 01865 241978.

Coming Back to Learning

Index

A

A levels 56
Academic qualifications 51
Access courses 21, **57**, 85, 144
Access funds 113
Accreditation of prior learning. . 64
Adult education 74
Adult education bursaries 115
Adult guidance services 30
Adult learners 10, **14**
Adult residential colleges -
  bursaries 115
Adult residential colleges 86
Advanced Highers 67
Advanced Modern
  Apprenticeships 82
Age Concern 34
Ageism 162
APEL 65
APL 64
Applications 151-4, 154
AS levels 56
Assistance with fees - further
  education 110
Assistance with fees - higher
  education 109

B

Basic skills 14, **19**
Basic skills education 53, 74
Benefits - studying while on 120
BTEC qualifications 58

C

CAB 125
Career Development Loans 117
Careers guidance services 30
CATS 45, **65**
CDLs 117

Certificate in Higher Education . 62
Charities - assistance with
  funding 119
Childcare facilities 148-150
Citizens Advice Bureaux 125
Colleges of further
  education **83**, 152
Community education 74
Correcting misconceptions 10
Course fees 106
Credit transfer 45, **65**, 156, 157

D

Dance and Drama Awards 115
Day release 45
DDA 35
Degrees **62**, 85, 90, 152
Diploma of Higher Education/
  DipHE **62**, 90
Disability - advice for students .. 35
Disability - financial help for
  students 112
Disability Discrimination Act ... 35
Distance learning 47, **48**, 94, 96
Drama courses - financial
  assistance 115

E

Education and Library
  Boards (N.I) 31
Educational Grants Advisory
  Service 125
Educational Guidance Service for
  Adults (N.I.) 31
Educational guidance services ... 30
Educational trusts 119
EGAS 125
EGSA 31
Employers - financial help 121
Employers 78, 121

167

Employment-based courses 49
Evening classes 43
Examination techniques 143
Ex-offenders - advice for 37

F

FE colleges 83
Fees - further education 107
Fees - higher education 106
Fees - open and distance
  learning 107
Flexible learning 47
Foundation degrees 62
Full-time education - financial
  assistance 104
Full-time study 42
Further education - financial
  assistance 110
Further education 73
Further education colleges 83

G

GCSEs 56
General National Vocational
  Qualifications/GNVQs 58
Government-funded training
  programmes - financial
  allowances 121
Graduate destinations 159
Graduate employment 22, **160**
Graduate recruitment 161
Graduate skills 161
Graduate Teacher Training
  Registry/GTTR 153

H

Hardship loans 113
Healthcare students - bursaries 113
Higher education - financial
  assistance 109
Higher education 73
Higher education colleges 89
Higher National
  Dip/Cert 58, 85, 90

Highers 67
HNDs **58**, 85, 90, 152

I

IAG services 30
ILAs 118
Independent learning **47**, 49
Independent providers 96
Individual learning accounts ... 118
Information, advice and
  guidance services 30

J

Jobcentres 32

L

learndirect 49, 72, **79**
Learner support services 144
Learning and Skills
  Councils 32, 75
Learning at work 77
LECs **32**, 81
Lifelong learning 8, 39, **156**
Local education authorities -
  advice on student finance .. 124
Local Enterprise Companies 32, 81
Lone parents - financial help ... 112

M

Mature students - financial
  help 112
Maturity 162
Modern Apprenticeships 82
Modular courses 44

N

NACRO 37
National Extension
  College 48, **98**, 108
National Learning Targets 8
National Qualifications
  (Scotland) 67

Index

National Training
  Organisations 30
National Vocational
  Qualifications 54
NEC **98**, 108
New Deal 80
NHS bursaries 113
NIACE 34
NIACRO 37
NMAS 153
Non-UK nationals - advice for ... 37
NTO National Council 30
NTOs 29
Nursery provision 149
Nurses and Midwives Admission
  System 153
NVQs 54

O

OCA 48, **98**, 108
Occupational skills 161
Open College of the
  Arts 48, **98**, 108
Open learning 47
Open University 48, **94**
Openings programmes 144
OU - fees 108
OU - financial assistance 110
OU 48, **94**
Overseas study 99

P

Part-time education - financial
  assistance 104
Part-time study 43
Postgraduate awards 63
Postgraduate finances 119
Postgraduate study 92
Professional bodies 38, **63**, 78
Profiles, list of 9
Publishers 165

Q

Qualifications 51
Qualification - equivalencies 52

R

RADAR 36
Refugee Council 38
Refugees - advice for 37
RETAS 38
Return to learn **43**, 74
RNIB 36

S

SACRO 37
Scholarships 115
Scottish qualifications 67
Scottish Qualifications
  Certificate 68
Scottish Vocational
  Qualifications 68
Self-confidence 16, **18**, 139
Self-employment 160
Short courses 45
Skill 36
Social context 16, **17**
Social Work Admissions
  System 153
Sponsorships 115
Standard Grades 67
Student counselling 145
Student loans 110
Study abroad 99
Study costs - other than fees 108
Study preparation 143
Study skills 144
Studying and training overseas
  financial assistance 123
Studying on benefits 120
SVQs 68
SWAS 153

169

T

Teachers - financial help while training 114
TECs 32, 81
Third Age Employment Network 35
Trade unions - financial assistance for learning 121
Trade unions 78
Trainee teachers - financial assistance 114
Training and Employment Agency (N.I.) 31
Training and Enterprise Councils 32, 81
Training for Work 81
Transport 150
Tutor-assisted independent learning 48

U

U3A 35, **77**
UCAS 153
UfI 79
UK NARIC 38
Universities 89
Universities and Colleges Admissions Service 153
University careers services 163
University for Industry 79
University of the Third Age 35, **77**

V

Vocational A levels 58
Vocational courses 24
Vocational qualifications 23, **51**
Voluntary organisations 33, **75**
Voluntary work 160

W

WbLA 81
WEA 76
Welfare services 150
Women into Science and Engineering/WISE 33
Women Returners' Network 33
Women's Training Network 34
Work-based Learning for Adults 81
Work-based training 24
Workers' Educational Association 76